"… must reading ...

— Dr. Robert D. Crane, Muslim author and former
White House policy advisor

"…For Dr. Imad-ad-Dean Ahmad…studying
the universe is an expression of faith.
Scientists and nonscientists alike should
appreciate the insights
in this passionate and lucid book."
— Dr. LeRoy E. Doggett, U.S. Naval Observatory

"Authored by a world-renowned astronomer
and astrophysicist, this volume is sheer
poetic testimony to the harmony (not conflict)
between religion and science.

"During the golden era of Islamic civilization
(8th to 15th century in Africa, Arabia,
and Persia) mathematics and science flourished
alongside poetry, calligraphy, and architecture.
As a slam made its way north and west into Spain,
France, Turkey, the Balkans, etc., it laid the
groundwork for Europe's Renaissance.

"Signs stands as a meticulously documented historical
record of scientific achievement in the medieval world."

— Kuumba Ferouillet Kazi, Black Collegian

SIGNS IN THE HEAVENS

In the name of God, the Beneficent, the Merciful

SIGNS IN THE HEAVENS

A Muslim Astronomer's Perspective
on Religion and Science

Imad-ad-Dean Ahmad, Ph.D.

amana publications

First Edition 1992

Second Edition 2006
amana publications
10710 Tucker Street
Beltsville, Maryland 20705-2223 USA
Tel: (301) 595-5999 / Fax: (301) 595-5888
E-mail: amana@igprinting.com
Website: www.amana-publications.com

Library of Congress Cataloging-in-Publication Data

Ahmad, Imad-ad-Dean, 1948-
  Signs in the heavens : a Muslim astronomer's perspective on
religion and science / by Imad-ad-Dean Ahmad.-- 2nd ed.
    p. cm.
  Includes bibliographical references.
  ISBN 1-59008-040-8
  1. Islam and science. 2. Astronomy--Religious aspects--Islam. 3. Astronomy--
Islamic Empire--History. I. Title.

  BP190.5.S3A37 2006
  297.2'65--dc22

                                                    2006003326

Printed in the United States of America by International Graphics
10710 Tucker Street, Beltsville, Maryland 20705-2223
Tel: (301) 595-5999 / Fax: (301) 595-5888

Website: igprinting.com
E-mail: ig@igprinting.com

DEDICATION

With all praise to God, the Exalted and Magnificent,
I gratefully dedicate this book to my wife Frances (*Hurriyyah*).

And among His Signs
Is this, that He created
For you mates from among
Yourselves, that ye may
Dwell in tranquility with them,
And He has put love
And mercy between your (hearts):
Verily in that are Signs
For those who reflect.

– Qur'an (30:21)

CONTENTS

ILLUSTRATIONS

ACKNOWLEDGMENTS

I am grateful to M. Abdus-Salaam Ahmad for his encouragement to undertake the first edition of this work. I thank the International Institute for Islamic Thought (IIIT) for allowing me access to their library, and to the American taxpayers for the Library of Congress. Drs. Jabir Taha Alalwani and Sayyid Syeed deserve acknowledgment for their encouragement. I am grateful to Patricia Nur Abdullah, James Kiefer, and Jamal Albarzinji for their comments on various portions of the first edition of this book, to Robert Crane for proof-reading the first draft of this edition and to Sarah Swick and Frances Eddy for proofreading the second edition. I am especially grateful to Dr. E. S. Kennedy for his valuable comments on the first edition and to N. Mahmood Ahmad for assistance with updating citations carried over from the first edition. I am deeply indebted to the Templeton Foundation for the grant that made possible the second edition of this work, and for their strong support of the study of religion and science in general. Prof. Owen Gingerich, Prof. Abdel-Haqq Guiderdoni and Dr. Munawar Anees provided valuable suggestions for the second edition. I would especially like to thank Prof. Gingerich, who intro-duced me to the serious study of the history of science, for his inspi-ration. It should go without saying that they bear no blame for any flaws in this book. The responsibility for all the research, assertions, analysis, and opinions is strictly mine and do not necessarily reflect the views of the John Templeton Foundation nor anyone else who assisted me in any way.

I am pleased to acknowledge the role my mother has played in introducing me to the religion of Islam and to the wonders of the world of the intellect. She has been a living demonstration of two important sayings attributed to the Prophet (peace be upon him): that the acquisition of knowledge is the duty of every Muslim male and female and that paradise lies at the feet of one's mother.

To God belongs all praise for anything good and worthwhile in this book, and to me belongs the blame for any errors and shortcomings; may God, and the reader, forgive me.

NOTE ON DATES, TRANSLITERATION, QUR'ĀNIC QUOTES, AND REFERENCES

Unless otherwise noted, dates are Common Era dates (i.e. Gregorian dates after 1582 and Julian dates before). Hijri (Islamic calendar) dates are normally indicated by the suffix A. H. (After Hijra, i.e., after the Prophet's flight from Mecca to Medina in 622 C.E.). When both dates are given separated by a slash, the Hijri date precedes the Common Era date. For example 657/1261 means 657 A.H. and 1261 C.E. (Julian).

I have tried to follow Library of Congress Bulletin 91 (Sept. 1970) in transliteration of Arabic characters, with the exception that dotted letters are underscored instead. Transliterated Arabic words will be indicted by italics: e.g., *ijtihād*. In cases of English words adopted from Arabic and proper names I will use the proper transliteration but without long bars, underscores and dotted separators (except in direct quotes and titles of works by others who use special markings). Thus, I have used Qur'an, not Qur'ān nor Koran. The Arabic definite article is uncapitalized except at the beginning of sentences. I have modified direct quotations of other works to conform to this system, but leave titles of other works as in the original cited.

All translations from the Qur'an are from A. Yusuf Ali's (1938) third edition unless otherwise noted. It was the last edition published during his lifetime, and contains material omitted from condensed editions such as the so-called "New and Revised" edition. In some cases I have reformatted the line breaks since Ali was constrained in the length of his lines by the fact that he was printing his English translation side-by-side with the Arabic text. As only the English translation is printed here, less frequent line breaks are more in keeping with the layout of this book and more concordant with the rhythm of the verses.

PREFACE

A popular subject of discussion in the modern West is the relationship between religion and science. Are they inherently incompatible or can they be reconciled? In the classical Islamic civilization science and religion were considered allies against paganism and superstition. Reconciliation was not an issue between two subjects that, to borrow a phrase from Thoreau, had never quarreled. This book advances the thesis that the myth of an incompatibility between religion and science is an accident of Western civilization, born out of its unique history.

The first edition of this book was written for the layman in nontechnical popular language about Islam and astronomy, but it was more fundamentally about the perspective of one modern Muslim astronomer on religion and science, since only God is completely objective. This second edition is the product of a research grant from the Templeton Foundation, and has benefited from the recommendations of three distinguished scientists who have been involved in the study of the history of science. In the fourteen years intervening between the two editions the quality of the discussion of the relationship between religion and science in Islamic civilization has risen to a more sophisticated plane. Ignorant dissertations based on the false premise that the Muslim world shared in the Dark Ages of Western Civilization are less prevalent. They have been replaced by thoughtful, though sometimes polemical, queries as to why Islamic science stagnated or declined while Western science blossomed into the Industrial Revolution and exponentially accelerated into the marvelous breakthroughs in research and technology that we witness on a regular basis today. Substantial new historical research has taken place supporting the thesis of this book so that it is now less novel, but, given recent world events, more impotant than ever. Responding to both the changing environment and to the recommendations of my colleagues, this new edition has become somewhat more academic than the first, yet still aims to be accessible to the lay reader.

In this book I present the attitudes towards science put forward in the Qur'an and the Prophetic traditions and by the great Muslim scholars of the classical era. I shall briefly review some of the scientific achievements of the golden era of Islamic civilization and in more detail discuss some important achievements in astronomy. I shall also try to show how the methodology of modern science was developed in the Islamic classical era and how advancements in science by the Muslims were the natural outgrowth of the Qur'anic foundations of Islam.

Several different topics will be addressed in this book: Prophet Muhammad's own experiences with astronomical phenomena; medieval Muslim scientific achievements; the current state of science in the Muslim world as demonstrated by confusion over the lunar calendar and the growth of Muslim pseudoscience; the harmony of faith and science in the Islamic tradition and the origin of the Western notion that these two concepts do conflict; the mounting dissatisfaction with the Ptolemaic system that lead up to what we know as "the Copernican Revolution."

Even in so dispassionate a field as physics, every scientist harbors affection for his own theories. He has a concern about what effect disproving his own previously published articles may have on future funding. Such emotions impede objectivity. Yet, objectivity still has some meaning even in the human realm.

Recently, a trend has emerged to transcend the Eurocentric bias of the Western educational establishment. To overcome that bias without replacing it with some new one is a worthwhile challenge. As a man raised with each foot in a different culture, I may be at an advantage in daring to rise to that challenge. In any case, I can think of no better project to try to bridge the gap of the European and Islamic cultures than a study of Islamic civilization's attitudes towards and contributions to science.

There are at least two themes in this book, each of which deserves a book of its own. For me, however, these themes are so closely related, that I think both deserve to be discussed together before attempting separate books to treat each in detail. Let the reader approach this book as a kind of overture to either or both of these themes or as an exploratory description of the relationship between them. The themes are that the view that there is such a conflict between science and religion is a myth that arose from the West's unique history and that in the classical Islamic era (when religion and science worked hand-in-hand) much progress was made in scientific research and techniques. The second of these supports the first (and main theme) by showing how a very religious culture was at the same time scientifically progressive. It is only fitting for a Muslim author to choose Islamic civilization to demonstrate this point. At the same time, candor requires a third theme, a counterpoint perhaps, that the modern Muslim world has fallen far from the golden era because Muslims have abandoned those principles and standards that made scientific progress possible. Which theme is in the fore varies as the reader progresses through the book. Perhaps, then, it will be helpful for me to outline what each chapter seeks to achieve in connection with the broader objectives of this book.

The first chapter notes that the perceived incompatibility between art and science is paralleled by the myth of an even deeper and fiercer opposition between (religious) faith and reason and that neither of these views is part of Islamic thought. An alternative view that the same God who revealed His message to the prophets gave us reason to be able to recognize His message and distinguish truth from error is put forth.

The second chapter puts forward the view that monotheism and reason are allies against pagan superstition. The demise of classical European science coincident with the incorporation of pagan elements into Western European Christianity is noted, as well as the coincidence of the rise of science in the Arabic language with the spread of Islam. The revitalization of European science at the time of its contacts with Islam is noted.

The third chapter enumerates the factors in Islam that were conducive to scientific development.

In the fourth chapter, three incidents in the life of the Prophet which may be related to the observation of astronomical events are examined to show that, despite his lack of scientific knowledge, his attitude was free from superstition and that he saw each incident as a sign of God's greatness rather than omens about mundane human affairs.

In the fifth chapter, we review some of the scientific accomplishments of the Islamic classical era with special emphasis (as befits an author who is an astronomer) on astronomy. We note that the most innovative scholars (like al-Biruni) were also the most pious.

In the sixth chapter we make some observations on the impact of Islamic science on the West. In particular, the "Great Chain of Being" and its authoritarian implications are explained. We show how Muslim astronomy eroded the foundations of the Great Chain of Being and paved the way for a scientific model in which all creation is equal under God. We contrast the persecution of Galileo and Bruno with the Muslims' attitude towards scientific scholarship in the classical era. Part of the European revolt against the anti-science of the authoritarian Church splintered off into an anti-religion movement that has left its mark on modern attitudes towards the relationship between religion and science.

In the seventh chapter, we look at the issue of the Islamic calendar and note the unscientific attitude with which modern Muslims have dealt with this problem. This is considered evidence of the decline of respect for science in recent Muslim history.

In the eighth chapter, we look at the rise of modern Muslim pseudoscience that treats the Qur'an, a book of guidance, as if it were a scientific textbook. Misleadingly called "Islamic science" this phenomenon has provoked a vehement reaction that has given the term "Islamic science" such a bad reputation that some are even denying that such a thing existed during the classical era, thus obscuring the very real contributions to scientific methodology that came out of the Islamic civilization.

The idea that the Muslims' willingness or unwillingness to resolve the confusion over the Islamic calendar in a scientific rather than authoritarian manner and that modern Muslims are unduly enamored of pseudoscientific claims about allusions to the natural world in the Qur'an leads directly to the ninth and final chapter, in which we enumerate the impediments to Muslim scientific growth: oppressive Muslim governments, colonial remnants of the faith versus reason dichotomy, and the absence of *ijtihād* (individual struggle for understanding). God does not change the condition of a people until they change themselves (Qur'an 13:11).

I should mention that there is a ghost that haunts this book. His name is well known to Muslims but will be unfamiliar to most non-Muslims who read this book. Yet even those who know his name are not generally familiar with the real essence of his teachings. He is Abu Hamid Muhammad ibn Muhammad at-Tusi al-Ghazali, and I wonder if ever so influential a man was so thoroughly misunderstood. He was the man who reconciled orthodox Islam and Sufism and who first advanced a truly modern theory of knowledge in which reason, experience, and authority were given balanced roles. Yet his teachings were so thoroughly misunderstood that instead of validating the rise of Islamic science they have been misread by non-Muslims as precipitating its decline and fall and misread by Muslims in a way that may have contributed to its decline and fall.

Al-Ghazali[1] had been a rationalist and a popular teacher of the philosophical school that thought that reason alone could lead to truth. Yet, his own keen intellect led him to the realization that this was simply not true. The realization that he was a hypocrite to teach

---

[1.] An exceptionally fine summary of al-Ghazali's life and teachings will be found in John Bowker, *The Religious Imagination and the Sense of God. Oxford,* Oxford University Press, 1978, 192-243.

his students that unaided reason could lead to truth when in his own heart it had lead him only to skepticism caused a psychological crisis and one day he stood before his class incapable of speech. He retired from teaching and from public life. His spiritual journey, described in his book *The Deliverance from Error* led him to the realization that while correct reasoning from correct premises could lead to truth, reason by itself could not ascertain which premises were valid and which were not. Experience and transmitted knowledge from reliable sources were required in order to know which premises were sound and which were suspect. He saw that the rationalistic philosophers in antiquity and in the Muslim world had accepted metaphysical speculation as axioms and he debunked them in his iconoclastic book *The Incoherence of the Philosophers*. Similarly, he saw that the authoritarian religious establishment had fallen prey to a similar error in accepting authority as the sole source of knowledge. And the radical Sufis too had made the error of relying on their mystical experience alone. One could be delivered from these errors by using reason, experience, and transmission from reliable sources as checks upon one another in arriving at the truth. The evolution of Islamic science was the gradual pragmatic development of this balance in the study of nature until what had been "natural philosophy" became modern science.

By training and by profession I am an astronomer. By ancestry and by choice I am a Muslim. I believe in Islam not because it happened to have been the religion of my ancestors, but because I have read the sacred Text, considered the arguments, and I am convinced. This book is written for the general reader, yet it reflects the vantage point of a man who is a Muslim and an astronomer for, after all, such a man wrote it. The limitations that the human condition places on objectivity, however, should never prejudice one's analyses. I am always open to refutation. I always want to hear the sincere and knowledgeable arguments on the other side, whether from other religious views or from critics of certain scientific theories that I have found persuasive. That is the best mechanism by which human beings, fallible as we are, may correct our errors. The other path, that of learning by experience, is also effective, but more painful.

The same God who revealed His Message to the prophets gave us reason in order to be able to recognize His Message and to distinguish it from fraudulent and foolish claims to divine guidance. As a Muslim scholar, commanded to engage in holy struggle (*jihād*) using my particular learning and skills, I must share my knowledge and understanding with others. By the grace of the one God (the God of Abraham and Jacob, Moses and Jesus, and Adam and Muhammad, peace be upon them all, and Who is called Allah in the Arabic tongue) and with the support of such of His servants as have led me to write the words contained herein, I offer this book to that end.

Imad A. Ahmad, Ph.D.

Bethesda, MD
October, 2005

CHAPTER 1

INTRODUCTION

Good thinking for an hour is better than divine service[2]
for one year. – *al-Ghazali*[3]

Look up at the sky on a clear, dark night. What is that feeling you get? I know no one who denies being moved by it. We differ in how we describe or explain our reaction, but surely it is, in every case, a feeling of awe, of wonder.

As a professional astronomer, I can tell you that I get a similar feeling at the moment of understanding of an equation that explains the motion of a pair of stars dancing in orbit around one another or of how the energy buried inside the heart of the sun is released in a burst when four hydrogen atoms are forcefully merged into a single helium atom. How different from Walt Whitman's self-description:

When I Heard the Learn'd Astronomer

When I heard the learn'd astronomer,
When the proofs, the figures,
    were ranged in columns before me,
When I was shown the charts and diagrams,
    to add, divide, and measure them,

---

[2] The term divine service here means formal ritual (*'ibādat*), since in Islam all good works, including "good thinking" constitute divine service in the broader sense.

[3] Abu Hamid al-Ghazali 1106-1111, *Al-Ghazzali's Ihya Ulum-id-Din*, Al-Haj Maulana Fazil-ul-Karim, trans. Lahore: Book Lovers Bureau, vol. 4 (1971), 453.

[4] Walt Whitman (1865), "When I Heard the Learn'd Astronomer," in *Leaves of Grass and Selected Prose*, John Kouwnhoven, ed. New York: Random House, 1950.

When I sitting heard the astronomer
   where he lectured
with much applause
   in the lecture-room,
How soon unaccountable
   I became tired and sick,
Till rising and gliding out
   I wander'd off by myself,
In the mystical moist night-air,
   and from time to time,
Look'd up in perfect silence
   at the stars.

In this poem we sense the literary intellectual who manifests contempt for scientists as discussed by C. P. Snow. Snow wrote of the "two cultures" that he saw in the West, one represented by the natural sciences and the other by the arts. He longed for a means of bridging the gap between them. He saw in the literary intellectuals an emotional resentment of technology.[5]

In contrast, Islam offers the example of the twelfth-century astronomer-poet Umar Khayyam. His reform of the Islamic calendar remains valid to this day, while 37 excerpts from his *Rubāyāt* are found in Bartlett's *Familiar Quotations*.[6]

The Muslim scholars of the classical, or golden, era of Islamic civilization (8th-15th centuries) did not suffer from the breach that Snow identified. The learned Muslim was equally at home

---

[5]"If we forget the scientific culture, then the rest of western intellectuals have never tried, wanted, or been able to understand the industrial revolution, much less accept it. Intellectuals, in particular literary intellectuals, are natural Luddites." C. P. Snow, *The Two Cultures and the Scientific Revolution.* New York: Cambridge Univ. Press, 1959, 23. The Luddites were 19th century bands of English handicraftsmen whose hatred for the machinery that was replacing them was manifested in destructive riots.

[6] See John Bartlett, Bartlett's Familiar Quotations. Boston: Little Brown, 1980.

with calligraphy as with medicine, with poetry as with astronomy. Learning of all sorts was of value. The concept of the "knowledge-able one" was highly respected, while that of the specialist was unknown.

After the European Christians took the border areas of Italy and Spain back from the Muslims, and trend-setting European scholars had the opportunity to attend some of the great universities developed under Islam, some European scholars adopted this broad attitude. Such scholars came to be known as "Renaissance men."

In the twenty-first century, the Renaissance man is rare. The perceived incompatibility between art and science is paralleled by the perception of an even deeper and fiercer opposition between faith and reason. Yet this, too, is not part of Islamic thought. Umar Khayyam was not only a poet and an astronomer; he was a Sufi and theologian, as well. Khayyam was well aware that the inductive techniques of the natural sciences could not be applied to the most fundamental questions of religion, but this did not mean that they in any way conflicted:

> Up from Earth's Centre through the Seventh Gate
> I rose, and on the Throne of Saturn sate,
>   And many a Knot unraveled by the Road;
> But not the Master-knot of Human Fate.[7]

The perceived opposition of faith and science is a product of the unique history of Europe. It emerged from the reaction of the medieval Western ascetic-mystical-hierarchical social structure centered on an authoritarian Church to its encounter with the remnant of Islam's moderate libertarianism, in which reason and faith are allies on the side of God against ignorance and uncertainty.

In opposition to asceticism (avoidance of earthly pleasures), Islam mandates moderation. God has not prohibited earthly

---

[7] *Rubāiyāt of Omar Khayyām* trans. by Edward Fitzgerald.

pleasure in itself. It is only forbidden to elevate it above submission to His will, or to prefer it to seeking His pleasure. In opposition to mysticism, Islam emphasizes the role of reason and experience in the acquisition and validation of knowledge. In opposition to the hierarchy of priestly church structures, Islam abolished the priesthood and established that every individual, male or female, is directly responsible to the Almighty.

Mysticism is used here to refer to the belief that the validity of knowledge acquired by "mystic experience" is exempt from critical scrutiny. It thus includes unintelligible doctrines, popular astrology, the occult, and alleged religious sources that contradict clearly demonstrable knowledge. The reader should be aware that I am not using the word in any of the other senses it may be used. For example, "mysticism" is commonly used by secular humanists to mean any religious experience or assertion. Such a characterization is an example of the fallacy about religion and science that this book is aimed at exposing and rejecting.

The Islamic attitude towards the mystic experience was well summarized by Iqbal. He noted that the abolition of priesthood, "the constant appeal to reason and experience in the Qur'an, and the emphasis that it lays on Nature and History as sources of human knowledge are all different aspects of the same idea,"[8] namely, "to create an independent critical attitude towards mystic experience.... Mystic experience, then, however unusual and abnormal, must now be regarded by a Muslim as a perfectly natural experience, open to critical scrutiny like other aspects of human experience."[9]

Human knowledge comes from a combination of reason, experience, and transmission from reliable sources. Revelation is not necessarily mysticism in this sense of the word, if it constitutes receiving the transmission from a reliable source. In the words

---

[8] Mohammad Iqbal, *The Reconstruction of Religious Thought in Islam*. Lahore: S.M. Ashraf, 1944, 101.

[9] Mohammad Iqbal, *Reconstruction*, 101.

of Thomas Paine: "No one will deny or dispute the power of the Almighty to make such a communication, if He pleases. But, admitting for the sake of a case, that something has been revealed to a certain person, and not revealed to any other person, it is a revelation to that person only. When he tells it to a second, and a second to a third, a third to a fourth, and so on, it ... is revelation to the first person only, and hearsay to every other."[10]

Muslims believe that there have been numerous recipients of revelation in mankind's history, including both Moses and Muhammad (Peace be upon them both). The text of that revelation to Muhammad was written down during his life and canonized by a committee chaired by his chief scribe under the review of a large population of people who had memorized the Book during the Prophet's lifetime.[11] This is more akin to a deposition than to hearsay, to respond in kind to Paine's legalistic language. The Pentateuch of Moses as we have it today were transmitted by an oral tradition extending over centuries before being canonized.[12] Paine's criticism, while inapplicable to the Qur'an, could be applied to the Islamic traditions known as the hadith. Although the historical scrutiny they underwent was more rigorous than was the case for the Pentateuch (see the discussion in Chapter 3), the hadith are, after all, just historical reports.

Belief in a revelation falls under my negative meaning of "mysticism" only if it is accepted in the face of contradictory knowledge of equal or superior standing, or if the claimant to revelation (or the chain of transmission) is not known to be reliable.

---

[10] Thomas Paine 1774, *The Age of Reason*. NY: Willey, no date, 8-9.

[11] See, e.g., Frederick M. Denny, "Islam, Qur'an and Hadith." In Frederick M. Denny and Rodney L. Taylor, *The Holy Book in Comparative Perspective*. Columbia, SC: Univ. S. Carolina, 1985, 84-108.

[12] See, e.g., Jonathan Rosenbaum, "Judaism, Totah, and Tradition." In Denny and Taylor, *The Holy Book*, 10-13.

The presumption that Revelation necessarily constitutes a form of mysticism, in the sense that I have defined the term, is yet another example of the Western assumption that faith and science conflict. Blind faith is not a pre-requisite for religious conviction. The Prophet himself was at first reluctant to believe that he had been chosen to be the recipient of revelation. He was profoundly shaken by his experience, and rushed home to his wife Khadija calling for her to cover up his trembling body. She consulted with a Christian cousin of hers who confirmed the substance and precedent of the revelation. After rationally examining his experience Muhammad came to realize its validity. For the Muslims who follow him, Muhammad's qualifications as a reliable source are well documented. (Unlike the other prophets, Muhammad is a figure in secular as well as religious history.) Finally, the Qur'an contradicts neither itself nor our other reliable sources of knowledge. Thus, the Muslim is not asked to suspend his critical faculty; on the contrary, the Qur'an asks the rejecters of Islam to use theirs. (See, e.g., 10:35, 21:65-67.) This is in contradiction to Draper's assertion that a "divine revelation must necessarily be intolerant of contradiction ... and view with disdain that arising from the progressive intellectual development of man."[13]

The word "mysticism" is also often used, by Sufis for example, to refer to direct communion with God. In this case, also, it is an example of "experience" for the person who experienced it. It falls under my negative use of the term if the person accepts the experience at face value, in contradiction to his other knowledge as, for example, schizophrenics are wont to do. It also falls under this negative meaning if a second person accepts a report of such an experience from an unreliable source. Thus, criticism of "mysticism" should no more be construed as a denial of the validity of the

---

[13] See John William Draper, 1876. *A History of the Conflict Between Religion and Science.* New York: D. Appleton, 1928, vi.

mystic experience than criticism of "rationalism" should be construed as a rejection of reason. The point in either case is that mystic experience should no more be exempt from critical examination than reasoning should be exempt from experimental verification.

The scholar of the classical Muslim civilization could be, and often was, both theologian and physicist. After all, the Author of Islam's Holy Book is the same as the Author of nature. Rather than fear contradictions between these two creations, the scholar looked forward to their mutual support. The religious ecstasy felt on reading the most exalted verses of the Qur'an is very much like the ecstasy felt in admiration of the stars. The quake within the soul that comes with the study of the Qur'an in the moment when a fundamental moral truth reveals itself is akin to the "Eureka"[14] of scientific understanding when one of the natural laws is laid bare.

To the average American or European raised on television and big city newspapers, who has gone to government schools and watched Hollywood movies, the claim that Islam is a practical, rational, and liberating religion must seem incredible. The serious Western student of Islamic history knows better. Yet, the facts have not made their way into the popular consciousness. Academic objectivity has, at best, been restricted to the boundaries of academic

---

[14] This expression originated with the exceptional Greek scientist Archimedes, a pioneer in the use of data from experimentation in developing scientific theories. The story goes that one day he had tired himself puzzling over how to determine whether a crown fashioned for the king was truly pure gold or had been abased with silver. From the weight of the crown he knew what its volume should be if it were all gold, but couldn't figure out how to determine its actual volume without damaging it. To relax, he retired to the baths and filled the tub to the top. When he entered it, the tub overflowed. Realizing with a flash that his body was displacing an equal volume of water he understood he could measure the volume of the ornate crown simply by placing it in water. Overcome with the discovery, he is said to have run home shouting "Eureka!" meaning "I have found it!" forgetting to put on his clothes first.

journals, although even there the evidence of bias due to geopoliti-
cal considerations that influence government grants, popular
acclaim, and media attention can be discerned.

A typically Eurocentric remark is that the "Middle Ages
were the age of faith, and to that extent they were unfavourable to
scientific speculation."[15] One would think the author is oblivious
to the fact that both faith and science were strong in the Muslim
world. Yet, he seems aware of the existence of a scientific culture
in the Islamic world, since he wonders what might be the source of
the translations from Arab works that entered Europe in the late
Middle Ages. In an essay on Francis Bacon, another writer puzzles
over Bacon's "quaint" language in referring to inhibiting mental
kinks in humans as "Idols." He seems unaware that Bacon is
emulating a style of terminology so common in Islamic circles as
to be clichés.[16]

Keeping Bacon's observations in mind, it is my aim to smash
one of the idols of the Western Market Place: the supposed antagonism between religion and science. The idea that the believer
must avoid science lest it erode his faith, or that the scientist must
avoid religion lest it weaken his analytical rigor, is foreign to Islam.
That is the theme of this book.

---

[145] M. Postan 1951, "Why was Science Backward in the Middle Ages?" In A Short History
of Science, ed. Jean Lindsay, New York: Anchor, 1959, 13.

[156] "Besides the tendency to accept on authority the dogmas of some prominent person or
sect, which Bacon calls "Idols of the Theatre," he enumerates three others. "Idols of the
Tribe" are certain unfortunate mental tendencies common to the whole human race: for
instance the tendency to notice facts which support one's beliefs and fall in with one's
wishes, and to ignore or pervert those which do not. Then there are "Idols of the Market
Place." These arise from the fact that many words and phrases embody the false beliefs
and inaccurate observations of our ancestors, and are thus, so to speak, crystallized errors
which we swallow unconsciously. Lastly, there are "Idols of the Cave." These are sources
of error or bias which are peculiar to each individual, depending on his particular
temperament and the special circumstances of his upbringing." C.D. Broad 1951, "Bacon
and the Experimental Method." In Lindsay, Short History of Science, 33.

Figure 1
The Andromeda Galaxy (Palomar Observatory)

We have indeed decked
The lower heaven with beauty
(In) the stars,–
– Qur'an (37: 6)

CHAPTER 2
SCIENCE & RELIGION

The science which is beneficial up to the end is the science of knowing God, His attributes and His works, His laws affecting this world and the hereafter. This is the science by which the blessings of the hereafter is gained. To exert oneself to the utmost of one's capacity to gain it falls far short of what is required, because it is such a sea of which the depth is unlimited. Those who search it are remaining constantly in its shores and edges. – *al-Ghazali*[17]

I do not know what I appear to the world, but to myself I seem to have been only a boy playing on the sea-shore, and diverting myself in now and then finding a smoother pebble or prettier shell than the ordinary, whilst the great ocean of truth lay all undiscovered before me. – *Isaac Newton*[18]

My thesis is that the belief that science and religion are opposed is a Western myth born of its unique history. We live in the post-colonial era when this myth, like many other Western ideas, has seeped into the numerous cultures that were so long under its influence. The belief that science and religious faith are incompatible is so widespread today that it seems intuitive. The view was articulated by Frazer, who asserted that science (like magic, he noted) seeks to control nature, while religion seeks to placate a superior Being, or beings, who control nature.[19] An alternative view is that the Supreme Being has

[17] al-Ghazali 1106-1111, *Ihya*, vol. 1, 54.
[18] See Bernard Darwin, *The Oxford Dictionary of Quotations (2nd Edition)*. London: Oxford University Press, 1959.
[19] James George Frazer 1922, *The Golden Bough*. New York: American Book Stanford Press, 1940.

provided man the ability (limited though it may be) to control nature and the command to do so in a moral manner. This is the actual Islamic view and may also be discerned in Judeo-Christianity, for example in the Biblical assertion that God gave man *dominion* over Creation. Yet Frazer's interpretation seems to be widespread in modern times. Cecil Schneer asserts that an example of this view was that "Benjamin Franklin was attacked as an atheist for his invention of the lightening rod."[20]

To explore the origin of this notion, we should free ourselves of any preconception that, by definition, religion and science are *inherently* opposed to one another. Let us try a few thought experiments.

Suppose that God created the heavens and the earth and devised the rules by which they operate. Suppose that this same God created reasoning beings to populate this earth and revealed to some of the more trustworthy among them His authorship of Creation and the moral principles under which these beings would prosper. Is there any reason that an objective study of the Creation itself by these reasoning beings must necessarily contradict the substance of the revelation? It should be apparent that the answer is no.

On the contrary, the discovery of a contradiction between the nature of the creation and the revelations about it would make us doubt either the correctness of the particular scientific theory contradicted or the validity of the presumed prophet (or perhaps both). There is no reason for us to question our faith in science *per se,* nor in revelation *per se.*

It is clear that there is no logical requirement that science and religion should conflict. Science is an exploration of the laws that govern nature (whether these laws were mandated by the Divinity or not) while religion mandates the moral laws by which men are

---

[20] Cecil J. Schneer, *Search For Order: The Development of the Major Ideas in the Physical Sciences from the Earliest Times to the Present.* New York: Grove, 1960, 5.

to govern their lives. Let us now examine the question of when and why religion and science have and have not historically conflicted.

In ancient times science was the ally of monotheism against pagan superstition. We can see this even in Western history. The pagan Greeks killed monotheistic Socrates for the "corruption" of the Athenian youth. His crime was to guide them into thinking for themselves. His student's student Aristotle[21] was a teacher of logic and physics and biology. He brought forth logical arguments for the existence of the "Prime Mover" but had no arguments to offer for the pantheon of lesser gods.

The Chaldeans and Babylonians were skilled in the science of astronomy. Their priests knew how to calculate the planetary motion to determine the months and seasons. The inclusion of this scientific knowledge in the category of special knowledge appropriate to a priesthood[22] kept the populace dependent upon the priests for guidance on when to hold their holy festivals and when to plant their crops.

If the people realized how perfectly obedient matter was to the laws of nature which God had authored, they might reject not only the priests, but the entire religious foundation on which the priestly power was built. According to the Qur'an, it was precisely in this manner that the prophet Abraham (peace be upon him) first arrived at the realization that there is only one God.

The idea that contemplation of the "signs in the heavens and the earth" leads to the conclusion of the existence of a single God is a

---

[21] Aristotle's teacher Plato was a student of Socrates. Aristotle's student Alexander the Great is believed by many Muslims to be the Zul-qarnain favorably mentioned in the Qur'an.

[22] *The Encyclopaedia Britannica* defines a priest as "the one who has a special and sometimes secret knowledge of ... acts that are believed to bridge the separation between the divine or sacred and profane realms." See Edwin O. James, "Priesthood," in the *Encyclopaedia Britannica, Micropaedia*, v. 14. Chicago: Encyclopaedia Britannica, Inc., vol. 14 (1980): 1007.

recurrent theme in the Qur'an. The specific experience of arriving at monotheism through astronomical observations of alleged deities is described by a particular passage of the Qur'an. Describing the experience of the Prophet Abraham, the Qur'an states:

So also did We show
Abraham the power
And the laws of the heavens
And the earth, that he
Might (with understanding)
Have certitude.

When the night
Covered him over,
He saw a star [*kawkab*]:
He said: "This is my Lord."
But when it set,
He said: "I love not
Those that set."

When he saw the moon
Rising in splendour,
He said: "This is my Lord."
But when the moon set,
He said: "Unless my Lord
Guide me, I shall surely
Be among those
Who go astray."

When he saw the sun
Rising in splendour,
He said: "This is my Lord;

This is the greatest (of all)."
But when the sun set,
He said: "O my people!
I am indeed free From your (guilt)
Of giving partners to God."

               – Qur'an (6:75-78)

Abraham taught to both branches of his growing family, Isaac
and Ishmael (peace be upon them) and their offspring, the important fundamental truth that he had learned. Nature is not under
the control of capricious and conflicting gods.[23] It follows the
grand design of a single Designer. This was not a mysterious secret
to be kept among a priesthood, but a practical fact of life which
was the responsibility of every individual to understand.

By the time of Jesus Christ (peace be upon him), the Jews were
subjected to a priestly class. The basic teaching of Abraham was
overshadowed by ethnic pride. The precise meaning of Jesus' message has become a controversial subject even among Christian
sects. Jesus taught the superiority of love and brotherhood over
legalism. Did this mean that he was overturning the religion of
Abraham? To the Muslims he was trying to reestablish it, not overthrow it. Jesus himself is reported to have said, "Think not that I am
come to destroy the law, or the prophets, I am not come to destroy,
but to fulfill."[24]

What the world calls Christianity is founded not so much on
the teachings of Jesus (which are affirmed in Islam) as on the
precepts of Paul (born Saul of Tarsus). The physicist Michael Hart,

---

[23] In a private communication (2003), Owen Gingerich has pointed out that this rejection
of the association of astronomical phenomena with Babylonian divinities is reflected in
the fact that "Genesis 1 does not mention the sun and moon by name, but the greater light
and the lesser light. This is because the words for sun and moon were Babylonian deities,
and the author of Genesis 1 wished to distance himself entirely from the Babylonian
mythology."

[24] Matthew 5:17.

explaining why he ranked Muhammad as the most influential person in history rather than Jesus (peace be upon them both), despite the fact that Christians have been more numerous than Muslims, wrote that Christianity had two founders, Paul and Jesus, and that it was Paul who wrote "a considerable portion of the New Testament" and "was the main proselytizing force for Christianity during the first century."[25]

Although born a Jew, Paul was a Roman citizen. Initially, he was a persecutor of the Christians. Then, he reported that he had a vision on the road to Damascus in which he saw Jesus speaking to him. He became the most dynamic advocate for what the world would come to know as Christianity.

Paul broke from the Judeo-Christianity of the early disciples who had known Jesus in life. Where they practiced Judaism with the acceptance of Jesus as the Messiah and the adoption of his spiritual message, Paul added the worship of Christ and, for non-Jewish converts, subtracted the observation of the Jewish laws.

Paul was knowledgeable in the polytheistic myths with which the Greeks were comfortable. He presented to the Gentiles what Muslims see as a hybrid of paganism and monotheism. He kept Jesus' Abrahamic message that God was one. Yet, he enchanted his pagan audiences with the claim that this unique God had, like their familiar Greek deities, sired a son, at once human and divine, through a human mother.[26]

Pauline Christians were confronted with three manifestations (or persons) of godhead which they had to reconcile with the doctrine of a single God: the Creator of all things (the Father); the Christ who had been incarnate among them (the Son); and the Holy

---

[25] Michael H. Hart, *The One Hundred: A Ranking of the Most Influential Persons in History.* New York: Hart, 1978, 47-48.

[26] Epistle to the Romans 1:3.

Spirit. Muslims, not assigning any divinity to the latter two, have nothing to reconcile. To them, only the Creator is God. Jesus, like Muhammad and the other prophets (peace be upon them all), is only a human messenger,[27] an example for men to follow and a teacher to heed. The Holy Spirit is usually understood to be the angel Gabriel, inspiring the human messenger with the divine message, but in any case is not God Himself.[28] The Pauline Christians, on the other hand, believe in the divinity of all three entities. The evolution of the mystical doctrine of Trinity was the result: three persons in one God.

The internal contradictions of this hybrid led to infighting among the Christians. Of the conflicting doctrines that contested with one another, the dispute between Arius and Athanasius is historically critical. It is also particularly pertinent to our thesis.

Arius (died 336) was a Christian priest from Alexandria, Egypt. He combined an emphasis on the oneness of God with a rational interpretation of the New Testament. To resolve the paradoxes of the Pauline doctrine, he characterized Christ as the most   perfect creature *in the material world* and considered him to be an *adopted* son of the one God.

Arius' doctrine was viewed as heretical. Reducing Christ's divinity to a secondary status was tantamount to denying it altogether. In opposition to Arius' view, the Alexandrian theologian Athanasius (*d.* 373) argued that Christ was the Son of God and *of the same substance as God the Father*.

Although he was not at the time a Christian, the Emperor Constantine called the Council of Nicaea in 325 C.E. to settle the dispute which was creating disorder in his empire. He imposed a state-sanctioned dogma on Christianity known as the Nicene Creed, which rejected the unitarian view. Arius refused to sign and

---

[27] See Qur'an 16:102 and 17:85.

[28] Qur'an 4:171 and 5:73. Also Abdullah Abbas Nadwi, *Vocabulary of the Holy Qur'an.* Chicago: Iqra International Educational Foundation, 1983, 236.

was declared a heretic. Eventually, Constantine converted to the religion he had helped to define and became the first Christian emperor, merging church and state.

By about 500 C.E., the Athanasian Creed was established. Christians were required to believe that God was one substance and three persons:

> ... the Father is Almighty, the Son Almighty, and the Holy Ghost Almighty, and yet they are not three Almighties but one Almighty, so the Father is God, the Son is God, and the Holy Ghost is God, and yet they are not three Gods but one God....

The *Encyclopaedia Britannica* reflects that this doctrine means "that the fundamental assumptions of the reality of salvation and redemption are to be retained and not sacrificed to the concern of a rational monotheism."[29]

Several critical things have all worked together here. The Church has adopted a mystical doctrine; the doctrine is to be imposed by the power of physical force; and the Church and State have become one. Mysticism, hierarchy and coercion are feeding on one another. The doctrine depends on mysticism to sustain it intellectually and appeals to a coercive structure to maintain it politically. Rational or independent inquiry threatens the doctrine. At the same time, the Church/State assumes its legitimacy from the asserted divinity of its foundation. Thus, any challenge to the doctrine is a challenge to the polity. Finally, the antagonism toward independent rational thought conspires with the authoritarian political structure's inherent encumbrance to productivity in the society. The absence of prosperity is not seen as a flaw in the social structure, but as a virtue by the ascetic standards of the religion. Thus, the ascetic-mystical-authoritarian network is completely integrated.

---

[29] Ernst W. Benz, "Christianity." In *Encyclopaedia Britannica*, Macropaedia, v. 4.

Western Europe plunged into the Dark Ages. With the embrace of asceticism, mysticism, and hierarchy, came the rejection of the material prosperity, learning, and democratic systems even such as the ancient world had been able to muster. Europe's own traditions of learning, such as the works of Aristotle and Pythagoras, vanished from her life.

> Few Christians regarded study of the natural world as of more than secondary, perhaps even tertiary, importance. Next to salvation and the development of basic Christian doctrine it was decidedly insignificant. There is no cause for alarm, Augustine pointed out, if the Christian "should be ignorant of the force and number of the elements.... It is enough for the Christian to believe that the only cause of all created things ... is the goodness of the Creator."[30]

As the Western Europeans were entering their age of ignorance, the Arabs were about to leave theirs. Arabia in the early seventh century was a land dominated by unlearned people. Although they had a talent for trade and poetry, horsemanship and tribal warfare, they were illiterate, characterized by the Prophet as a people "who can neither write nor count." They were also morally destitute, with no respect for women, practicing ritual human sacrifice and slaughtering female infants. Their knowledge of science was negligible. They could not calculate their own calendar reliably. This left a great opportunity for mischief in political affairs.

By Arab tradition, four months were sacred and warfare in them strictly forbidden. The leadership of the tribes would take advantage over calendrical confusion to insert leap months in such a way as to make the war permissible when it was to their advantage. This would have an effect opposite to the purpose of the sacred months. Instead of preventing war during the holy seasons, a new cause for dispute was made.

---

[30] David C. Lindberg, *Science and The Early Church.* In David C. Lindberg and Ronald L. Numbers, *God and Nature.* Berkeley: U. of California Press, 1986.

Into this world the Prophet Muhammad was born. Muhammad was as unlettered as his people and could neither read nor write. Like the prophets before him, however, he received a revelation from God, passed on by the angel Gabriel, which transformed the lives of those who accepted it. The Qur'an (*Qur'ān* is Arabic for "reading" or "recitation") that he passed on to his companions called upon mankind to reject the false gods it worshiped. It contained no excuse for the worship of any human being, institution, or force of nature. Instead, it commanded the worship of God alone. Also, it appealed to human reason and experience in making that command. It offered as reward success in this life *and* in the next. It ridiculed the pagan superstitions by exposing their internal contradictions and their departure from sound observation of the signs of God around us. It praised the Christians and Jews for being closer to God than the pagans. Yet, it criticized Christianity for assigning divinity to Jesus and for propagating asceticism and the mystical doctrine of Trinity. It criticized the Jews for rejecting their own prophets' call to obey God and instead seeking to turn their religion into an exaltation of their own ethnic group above the rest of the brotherhood of mankind.

The message of Muhammad captured the hearts of the Arabs and of their neighbors. Within a hundred years it had spread from Spain to India. Carlyle writes: "As if a spark had fallen, one spark on what seemed a world of black unnoticeable sand; but lo! the sand proves an explosive powder, blazes high from Delhi to Grenada!"[31] Rose Wilder Lane remarked that this

---

[31] Thomas Carlyle, *Heroes and Hero Worship*. Chicago: A.C. McClurg & Co., 1897, 93.

explosion "created the first scientific civilization."[32] Dreyer wrote that "under Islam there was an entire absence of that hostility to science which distinguished Europe during the first half of the Middle Ages."[33]

The Prophet taught a pro-science message in three respects. First, the acquisition of knowledge was not merely the right of every individual, male or female, but a *duty*. This contradicts the notion that knowledge is the province of the priests. In Islam, the priesthood was abolished. Second, the acquisition of knowledge was empirical as well as reflective. That is, the Qur'an specified that we have a duty to observe God's signs in the heavens and on earth. Third, science is not to be purely abstract but applied as well. Practical action and improvement of life on earth is part of the Muslim's charge. The Muslim is not in the position of a helpless victim in need of *salvation*, but of a responsible agent who needs to act in order to achieve success (*falāh*) in this world and the next.

Al-Ghazali, the twelfth-century scholar who reconciled Sufism and orthodox Islam, wrote in his *Revival of Islamic Knowledge* that scientific research could only be held blameworthy if one of three conditions applied: (1) if it harmed others, (2) if it harmed the acquirer, or (3) if it is futile or useless. Al-Ghazali made it clear that by the last condition he was not opposing pure science (which he praised) but denouncing "for example, learning of trivial sciences before the important ones, learning of subtleties before fundamentals."[34] For

[32] Rose Wilder Lane, *Islam and the Discovery of Freedom*. Beltsville, MD: amana, 1997, 13. Muslims believe that all monotheistic religions in their uncorrupted form put forth essentially the same teaching as Islam. From the Islamic perspective, the failure of Medieval Europe to develop a scientific civilization is attributable to Christian departures from the actual teachings of Jesus. Judaism, on the other hand, retains its original pro-reason attitude. Its failure to develop a lasting scientific civilization has a different explanation: its golden era lasted for only two generations, the kingdoms of David and Solomon. The reason for its fall is not due to any lack of respect for science, but for other reasons that shall be touched upon in Chapter 9.

[33] J. L. E. Dreyer 1906, *A History of Astronomy from Thales to Kepler*. New York: Dover, 1953, 249.

[34] al-Ghazali 1106-1111, *Ihya*, 47.

example, Islam does not approve of disputes over how many angels may dance on the head of a pin.

In the seven hundred years that followed the Prophet's establishment of an Islamic community, the rational, practical and egalitarian religion produced a civilization as bright as the corresponding civilization in Europe was dark. The sciences of the civilizations which the Muslims inherited were not merely preserved, as American schoolbooks would have you believe, but digested, expanded upon and they flowered into whole new sciences.[35]

Until about 800 C.E., Western Europe was in the deepest pit of the Dark Ages. After Charlemagne's unsuccessful skirmishes against the Muslim civilization in Spain, Western Europe began to experience a cultural rebirth. Yet, European science remained insignificant until a stronger and more influential interaction with the Muslim world took place centuries later.

In the twelfth century, Europe was still in an unhappy state. The Church was divided and the continent racked by warfare. The weaker of the two Popes claiming authority at the time made a call to holy war: to a Crusade against the Muslims. While the Pope's actual motives in initiating the Crusades are disputed, there is no doubt about the results. The other Pope was eliminated; the bloodshed in Europe diminished; "and during the absence of the fighting men, The Church became The Authority."[36]

The Pope's plan to turn European turmoil against an external enemy eventually wrought an unanticipated consequence of historic proportions. It forced Europeans into contact with an alien

---

[35] Contributions of Islamic civilization to Western civilization can be found in John William Draper, *A History of the Intellectual Development of Europe*, 2 vols. New York: Harper & Brothers, 1876. Chapter 2 of Volume II is of particular interest; George Sarton, *Introduction to the History of Science. I. From Homer to Omar Khayyam*. Washington DC: Carnegie Institute of Washington, 1927; and George Sarton, *Introduction to the History of Science. II. From Robert Grosseteste to Roger Bacon*. Washington DC: Carnegie Institute of Washington, 1931.

[36] Lane, *Islam*, 30.

ideology and a civilization rich in scientific knowledge. The contact with Islamic civilization brought about a rebirth of interest in scientific thought in Europe. Europe's eventual conquest of the border regions of Spain and Italy sparked the Renaissance[37], and the adoption of a number Islamic ideas that directly conflicted with medieval notions.

The three attitudes that Islam had about scientific knowledge were the importance of the observational aspect, that it belonged to everyone, and that it had practical applications; these were a challenge to the medieval European attitudes. Their impact was enormous.

The first of these attitudes towards knowledge to infiltrate Europe was the importance of experimental techniques in the scientific process. Thus, we find Albert Magnus and Roger Bacon, having been thoroughly exposed to Islamic influences, employing experimental techniques in the thirteenth century. Sarton has noted that, in this respect, Ibn al-Haytham influenced not only Bacon, but even Kepler.[38] The Church itself was more resistant to this attitude. Magnus' student St. Thomas Aquinas wrote in an Aristotelian style, emphasizing pure reason rather than induction (see Chapter 6), and even in Galileo's time Church scholars were still suspicious of instruments like the telescope.

Next to infiltrate was the idea that knowledge belongs to the masses. Thus, we find Dante, at the Italian contact point with Islamic civilization, writing in the vernacular. Later, when Islamic Spain fell to the European Christians, Cervantes would follow suit writing in Spanish. There is evidence of the Islamic connection beyond the geographical circumstances. Dante's heaven and hell employ allegories

---

[37] Stanwood Cobb, *Islamic Contribution to Civilization*. Washington, D.C., Avalon Press, 1963.

[38] George Sarton, *Introduction to the History of Science*. I, 721.

taken from Muhammad's *mi'rāj* (the ascension into heaven)[39] as well as cosmological concepts picked up from al-Farghani.[40]

The practical applications of science in Europe came quickly and the power of those applications increased exponentially. In this respect, the transition from the Islamic world was seamless.

Along with the introduction of modern applied science to Europe, however, has arisen a peculiar debate about the propriety of using technology to relieve humanity of the pain of its toil and suffering—one that has no precise parallel among Muslims. It is not that Muslims have no concerns about risks associated with technology. It is rather that the theme so often struck in the West that the very prospect of improving life on earth into increasingly greater comfort is in itself a moral threat I have not seen among Muslims. Consider the issue of in vitro fertilization. While Muslims are as concerned as anyone in the West about the risks that such technology may lead to an increase in the number of children without proper families, no Muslim authorities share the Catholic church's categorical objection to the process that would prohibit even married couples from using it to overcome fertility problems.

To the ascetic European-style religion, the establishment of a materially comfortable life on earth is a sinful rejection of the religious doctrine that earth is a place of misery and woe from which salvation must be sought. There is a common understanding of Genesis 3:17-19: "...Cursed is the ground for thy sake; in sorrow shalt thou eat of it all the days of thy life; Thorns also and thistles shall it bring forth to thee; and thou shalt eat the herb of the field; In the sweat of thy face shalt thou eat bread, till thou return to the ground...." This picture is challenged by the Qur'anic view that man is not a fallen creature in disgrace and need of salvation, but a volitional creature on trial and in need of guidance. The earth is the stage

---

[39] See Miguel Asin, *Islam and the Divine Comedy*. New Delhi: Goodword, 2001.

[40] See Dreyer, *A History of Astronomy*, 235-6.

on which man must apply his rational faculties for the betterment of himself and the human family:

> Your Lord is He
> That maketh the Ship
> Go smoothly for you
> Through the sea, in order that
> Ye may seek of His Bounty.
> For He is unto you Most Merciful.
>   – Qur'an (17:66)

The material prosperity that came from scientific progress posed a dilemma for a society that had philosophically prized poverty and held affluence in contempt. The Protestant Reformation resolved this dilemma by advocating a work ethic that found prosperity unobjectionable, even praiseworthy, provided it was not used for enjoyment, but rather re-invested in greater productivity. Islam, spared any such dilemma, never adopted this attitude, applying instead the standard of moderation to matters of work and enjoyment.

> O Children of Adam!
> Wear your beautiful apparel
> At every time and place
> Of prayer: eat and drink:
> But waste not by excess,
> For God loveth not the wasters.
>   – Qur'an (7:31)

With the arrival of the "modern" era to Europe, scientific inquiry and material prosperity experienced a revival. So, also, did the doctrine of Arius, especially in the philosophy of Isaac Newton and the Unitarian movement. We shall return to this in Chapter 6. For now, we note that the complex conflict between those scholars seeking to incorporate the elements of natural religion into Christian thought against those seeking to defend the evolved orthodoxy was interpreted by some nineteenth century writers like Draper and White as a war between religion and science.[41] Although historians in more recent times have questioned this nineteenth-century view,[42] there is still a widespread impression among the general public that an inherent conflict does exist between religion and science.

---

[41] See John William Draper, *A History of the Intellectual Development of Europe*. And Andrew Dickson White, *A History of the Warfare of Science with Theology in Christendom*, 2 vols. New York: Appleton, 1896.

[42] See, e.g., Lindberg and Numbers, *God and Nature*.

Figure 2
Jupiter and its Galilean Satellites (NASA)

Praise be to God,
The Cherisher and Sustainer of the Worlds. . . .
– Qur'an (1:2)

CHAPTER 3
THE SIGNS OF GOD

Obaid said: Inform me of a wonder which you have seen of the Prophet. At this Hazrat Ayesha began to weep and said: All his works are wonderful. He came to me in his appointed night, even my body touched his body. Then he said to me: O Ayesha leave me, will you, [to] worship my Lord? He then went to a water skin, performed his ablution and began to weep in his prayer so much that the tears wetted his beard. Then he prostrated so much that the ground underneath him became wet. Thereafter he laid on one of his sides. Bilal came to call him for Fajr prayer and saw that he was weeping. He asked: O Prophet of God, why do you weep? Your past and present sins have been forgiven. He said: Woe to you, O Bilal! Who will prevent me from weeping? God revealed this verse this very night: In the creation of the heavens and the earth and in the changing of nights and days there are surely signs for the intelligent [Qur'an 3:190]. Then he said: Woe to him who reads this verse and does not ponder. – *al-Ghazali*[43]

The ancient world made tremendous achievements in science. As we have mentioned, that great heritage was for a long time lost to medieval Europe. Although the achievements of the Greeks and other pagan societies–the Babylonians, the Chaldeans, the Hindus–were impressive, they differed from Islamic science in an important way that brings them short of what we mean when we speak of modern science.

---

[43] Al-Ghazali, *Ihya*, vol. 4, 454.

Most Hellenic scholars were attracted to a deductive method of thought. By this, we mean that they thought that true knowledge could be achieved by pure reason alone. As if a scholar could lock himself in an ivory tower and, by sheer but careful thought, could deduce the structure of the universe.

Greek science differs from modern science in its epistemology.[44] Epistemology is the theory of knowledge, the answer to the question "How do you know what you know?" The stereotypical ancient scientist is Aristotle. Aristotle identified the essence of doing science as understanding why everything is as it is on the principle that it could be no other way. This concept is a reflection of an epistemology that I call rationalism. "Rationalism" is a word that gets used with many different meanings to different people. I want it to be very clear, therefore, that when I use the term "rationalistic science" I mean neither science that employs reason nor science that insists upon an adherence to reason. I mean a science in which reason is considered to be the dominant means for the acquisition of knowledge, in which reason overshadows if not completely replaces any other means of the acquisition of knowledge. What this meant to the ancient Greeks was that if you began with the correct axioms, the correct premises, the correct starting points, that, by reason alone, you could completely deduce the nature of the universe. Modern science doesn't work that way.

Modern science works by what some call "the Scientific Method" and others say should be called "the scientific methods." Some call it "inductive science" or "inductive reasoning." Any really intelligent high school student could explain to you that modern science involves not only reason, but also observations of

---

[44] The next six paragraphs are excerpted from a previously published article, Imad-ad-Dean Ahmad, "Islamic Contributions to Scientific Methods." *The Journal of Faith and Science Exchange* IV (2000): 27-30.

THE SIGNS OF GOD   31

experiments. The idea is that our reason must match our observation and our theories must be tested by our experiments, and that there is a great cycle in which theories inspired by observations are tested by experiments that lead to refined theories to be refined or overthrown by yet further experimentation or observation.

Yet, this is only two-thirds of the story. There is another element of modern science that never gets mentioned. Since the existence of this third element as a method of modern science is undeniable, I cannot help but think that the reason that it never gets mentioned is that people want to contrast modern science against the way of thinking that dominated the Middle Ages–and here I mean the Western European Middle Ages–that was more authoritarian. What Western European moderns viewed Medieval thinking to be was parodied by Moliere in the play *La Malade Imaginaire* (the Hypochondriac) with the character of a doctor who still had a medieval way of looking at things, and the doctor would begin every analysis with the introduction: "Aristotle *dit*" ("Aristotle says"), as if the fact that Aristotle said something constitutes a proof. Yet, referral to authority is an important element of the acquisition of scientific knowledge. Most of what any scientist knows about his discipline, he has read in the scientific literature. Individual scientists do not check every detail of every theory upon which their own work is based. Scientists do not attempt to reproduce every experiment on which their data is based, nor do they duplicate every observation upon which their work is based. Scientists resort to the scientific literature and they incorporate, adopt and build upon what they find there. Yet there is an important difference between the way the modern scientist uses the scientific literature and the treatment the medieval scholars approached the sacred or ancient scientific texts, the "ancient wisdom." Above all, the modern scientist approaches the literature critically. He does not presume that it is beyond question. Secondly, he requires proper citation.

Modern philosophers understand that logic is nothing more than a means of manipulating symbols. There can be no meaning assigned to the symbols by logic. The only reason we can make meaningful statements about the world using logic is that our experience has allowed us to associate meanings with the symbols. If we look around us we discover that there is much we know that we do not reason from first principles. There are things we can only know by transmission. For example, I know that Thule, Greenland exists. I do not know this by experience, for I have never been there, and I certainly could not derive its existence from first principles. No simple set of self-evident axioms will allow me to prove the existence of Thule, Greenland by some complex but rigorous chain of reason. What has happened is that honest and sane people I have known who have been there have told me of their experiences, and I have no reason to doubt them. On the contrary, maps by reliable mapmakers confirm their claims.

Similarly, we have to rely on reason as well as experience. Walking through the desert I may perceive a lake in front of me, but if the circumstances are those under which reason dictates that a mirage is possible, I am justified in doubting the evidence of my own eyes. Add to this the evidence of transmission from a reliable source–say a map that shows there is no lake in this place, then I may rely on that map to correct my erroneous sensory experience. When we become skilled at testing these three sources of knowledge against one another, then we know that we are getting close to the truth and we may rely upon it. This is the epistemology of al-Ghazali and we can see its parallels with the methods of modern science.

You can find, even in ancient times, individual scientists who seem very modern in their approach, (Archimedes, for example, has always impressed me in this way). Nonetheless, the first civilization to nurture and produce a modern approach to science in which all three of these elements (reason, experiment or observation, and critically approached and properly cited authority) was the classical Islamic civilization. It was developed there in a gradual way. Westerners tend to look at it as a "scientific revolution" that took place in Western Europe, was very abrupt, and very shocking in its effects on the culture. My understanding is that the West discovered it through their contact with Islam, and because it was thrust upon them so suddenly it did indeed have a shocking effect on Western society. In the Muslim world it evolved gradually and produced no such shock.

If it were truly the case that everything is as it is because it could be no other way, then all scientific knowledge could be rationally deduced from self-evident axioms and observation would play no important role beyond a contemplative stimulus to rational thought. Modern science, however, depends upon observations and experiments as well as rational thought in a critical way. In addition, modern science depends on the transmission of accumulated knowledge through a refereed and properly cited literature. These additional factors evolved during the classical Islamic civilization. Al-Ghazali, who critiqued Greek science for inadmissibly mixing metaphysics with physics in his book *The Incoherence of the Philosophers*, documented the importance of these additional factors in his *Deliverance from Error*. The three-legged epistemology in which reason, empirical data and authoritative citation check and reinforce one another is the real distinguishing mark of modern scientific methods. This modern method of engaging in scientific research did not emerge mysteriously and instantaneously in the modern West. From its precursors in ancient science, as we shall show, it evolved into a systematic method of research during the classical Islamic civilization, refined by scholars like al-Biruni, Ibn Haytham, and Ibn ash-Shatir, encouraged by certain Islamic teachings.

In harmony with their rationalist epistemology, the Greeks looked upon mathematics as the queen of the sciences.[45] Astronomy seemed a bit tainted in comparison. The astronomer dealt with stars and planets, objects that were of the physical world. Mathematicians dealt with circles and numbers, wonderful objects from the realm of pure ideas.

Despite their intuitive awareness that there was a difference between the "purity" of mathematics and the rest of the sciences, they believed that the scientific facts about the universe could be derived by reason alone. Thus, the Pythagoreans' mathematical idea that the circle is the purest of shapes led to the derivation that planets move in circles. Of the shortcomings of this conception and how the Greeks dealt with it, we shall speak later.

In contrast, the Muslims considered astronomy the queen of sciences. The paths of the planets through the sky were things that you could see with your eyes. For the Muslim, those paths had to be carefully measured so that the mathematical theories that appeared to explain them could be tested.

> Do they not look
> At the sky above them?–
> How We have made it
> And adorned it,
> And there are no
> Flaws in it?
>   – Qur'an (50:6)

---

[45] "Because numbers and forms appeared to the Greeks as the only ideal and perfect things in a naughty world, they became the focus for a religious mystique. Legend has it that Pythagoras was the founder and leader of a secret society, a religious fraternity, dedicated to the study of the number-universe. To the Pythagoreans numbers and forms were real. Things were only crude approximations of these pure ideas. It was as natural for them to turn their backs on society and the everyday world and to devote themselves to the study of numbers as it was for the theologians of the Middle Ages to immerse themselves in the study of scripture and the writings of the Fathers." Schneer, *The Search,* 22

[Blessed be] He Who created
The seven heavens
One above another:
No want of proportion
Wilt thou see
In the Creation
Of (God) Most Gracious.
So turn thy vision again:
Seest thou any flaw?

    – Qur'an (67:3)

The implication is that any discrepancy between our understanding of the harmony between God's natural laws and our observations of their fulfillment is due to a failure of our understanding, not to any imperfection in the nature of material reality. Either our theories are in error or our observations are faulty. The material universe obeys God's commands without question, and those commands are perfect and beautiful. Thus, "Al-Battānī said that the science of the stars comes immediately after religion as the noblest and most perfect of the sciences, adorning the mind and sharpening the intellect, and that it tends to recognize God's oneness and the highest divine wisdom and power."[46]

The Platonic attitude reflects a view that form and matter are at odds, while the Islamic view reflects a view of unity between form and matter. Plato believed in a dichotomy of the realm of forms from the realm of the physical world and "systemized the Pythagorean mystique into the formal philosophy of idealism."[47] This has been understood as the distinction between the ideal and the material. To the Muslim, God's formal law is obeyed by matter and reflected in it:

---

[46] A. Pannekoek, *A History of Astronomy*. London: George Allen and Unwin Unl., 1961, 167.

[47] See Schneer, *The Search*, 29.

Do they seek
For other than the Religion
Of God?–while all creatures
In the heavens and on earth
Have, willing or unwilling,
Bowed to His Will
(Accepted Islam),
And to Him shall they
All be brought back.

    – Qur'an (3:83)

Plato felt that the corporeal world could only imperfectly reflect the perfection of ideals in the mind of the Deity. The incorporation of this metaphysics into Christianity was described by Gibbon in this way:

> ... the three *archical* or original principles were represented in the Platonic system as three gods, united with each other by a mysterious and ineffable generation; and the Logos [the Word, reason or first cause] was particularly considered under the more accessible character of the Son of an Eternal Father, and the Creator and Governor of the world.[48]

Gibbon noted that such an attempt to reconcile the imperfect creation with the perfect Creator "might please, but could not satisfy, a rational mind." This polytheistic system influenced Christian theology when "the name and divine attributes of the Logos" were confirmed by the celestial pen of Saint John.[48]

---

[48] Edward Gibbon 1776, *The Decline and Fall of the Roman Empire, volume I*, in *Great Books, v. 40*. Chicago: Encyclopedia Britannica, Inc., 1952, 307.

There were many "gospels" (collections of traditions about the life and teachings of Jesus, peace be upon him) circulating among the early Christians. At the same Council of Nicaea discussed in the previous chapter, a determination as to which gospels were to be approved as canonical and which rejected as apocryphal was made. *The Gospel of Barnabas,* which, if we may judge by the fifteenth-century Italian translation by Fra Marino,[49] was a strongly unitarian document, was rejected, along with many others. The gospels of Mark, Matthew, Luke and John were canonized. Of these four, the last is the most separated from the actual time of Jesus in its origin. It is strikingly dissimilar from the other three in both content and style. Its metaphysical approach to the significance of Jesus' teachings lends itself well to the Gnostic school.[50] Its acceptance as one of the canonical gospels incorporates Platonic thought into the doctrines of Christianity.

If, as Plato taught, this material world is only the ghostly shadow of the real world of ideas, then it would seem foolish to test the validity of an idea by trying to observe whether or not it is followed in the real world. For the Platonist, the senses are unreliable. The empirical route to knowledge is not the straight one. If I should see a dog that has lost one of its legs, shall I permit this to shake my understanding that a dog is a four-legged animal?

---

[49] This has been rendered into English by Lonsdale Ragg and Laura Ragg, *The Gospel of Barnabus*. Cedar Rapids, IA: United Publishing, 1980.

[50] Gnosticism constitutes a claim of special knowledge of the secret mysteries. Gnostic metaphysics in the Christian context has denied the existence of evil. The doctrine is considered heretical by mainstream Christianity, but has been revived in teachings found in the Christian Science denomination. See Ismāil Raji al-Faruqi, *Christian Ethics: A Historical and Systematic Analysis of Its Dominant Ideas.* Montreal: McGill University Press, 1967. For a discussion of the responsibility of Gnosticism for the Gospel of John and other parts of the Pauline and Apostolic writings, see Rudolph Bultmann, *Theology of the New Testament.* tr. by K. Grobel, London: SCM Press, 1958.

This attitude could be seen in the actual writings of the archetype of rationalism, Aristotle. Aristotle declared that women have fewer teeth than men because they have smaller mouths.[51] Why did he not look in his wife's mouth and see that he was in error? As with the three-legged dog, it appears that he did not want irrelevant material facts to confuse the issue where his beautiful reasoning was concerned.

Al-Ghazali pointed out hundreds of years ago that we have three sources of knowledge: experience, reason, and transmission from reliable sources. In most cases, what we know is due to a complex interaction of all three of these. Some knowledge, as for example that of the existence of an afterlife, can only stem from transmission.[52] Experience does not suffice, for most of us will die only once. Reason alone cannot resolve the question for it has no premises on which to base its conclusions. Some knowledge, such as the rules of logic, can be derived by reason alone. For some things, the mere experience is sufficient. For example, neither rational analysis nor the commentary of others will fundamentally alter the affection a mother feels for her child.

In modern science all three sources of knowledge play a role. Both experiment (or observation) and reason (theory) are used and serve as checks upon one another. This is what we mean by induction, sometimes called the scientific method.[53] In addition,

---

[51] Bertrand Russell, *The Impact of Science on Society*. London: Allen & Unwin, 1952, 7.

[52] I stress the importance that transmission be from a reliable source. This is how actual revelation is distinguished from mysticism as I use the term here (see pp. 4*ff.*). The genuineness of Muhammad's prophetic experience is attested to by his own resistance to believe in it. Contrast his attitude described on page 6 with the uncritical acceptance of their "mystical experiences" which is evidenced by spiritualists, drug-users and schizophrenics. The fact that a messenger or a message *claims* to be from God is not sufficient cause for its acceptance. If it contradicts the rest of our knowledge, whether from experience, reason, or more reliable authorities, it must be rejected.

[53] It would be more appropriate to say scientific methods since there are many techniques used in modern inductive science.

transmission plays a role, as scientists depend upon one another for data, for alternative theoretical models, and for critical review. Yet, no scientist will accept the reports of another that irreconcilably contradicts his own experiments. Science avoids subjectivity and error by such requirements as repeatability. It is not enough that one scientist obtains a certain result from an experiment or is able to make a certain observation. Any scientist must be able to obtain similar results under similar circumstances.

Modern inductive science is a process by which all these sources of knowledge interact. Observations beget theories and further observations check theories. This differs from the deductive method in which reason alone attempts to derive knowledge from first principles.

While there is some dispute among Western scholars as to whether the experimental techniques associated with induction are the creation of the modern or the ancient world, until recently they had attributed their development solely to European scholars. I suggest that the development of induction as practiced in the natural sciences was a gradual process and that a significant part of it took place during the classical Islamic era, spurred on by the Qur'anic attitude we have discussed in this chapter.

> The emergence of this new dimension can best be seen in optics, in the work of Ibn al-Haytham (Alhazen).... [H]is successors adopted experimental norms in their research on optics – for example, their research on the rainbow.

> ... [S]ome of Ibn al-Haytham's experiments were aimed not simply at verifying qualitative assertions, but also at obtaining quantitative results....[54]

---

[54] In particular Kama ad-Din al Farsi (d. ca. 1320) simulated a rainbow through the use of a glass sphere. Toby Huff, *The Rise of Early Modern Science: Islam, China, and the West*. New York: Cambridge, 2003, 210.

After this lengthy preface, we are ready to look at an example from astronomy. Have you ever looked closely at a spinning top? The top spins rapidly around its axis. If the axis is tilted away from a vertical line out of the earth's surface, you must have noticed that the axis of the top slowly circles around that vertical line. This is called precession. In the same manner the North Pole of the earth precesses and points at different places as the centuries pass. At this moment, it points towards Polaris (the North Star). It is moving ever closer to Polaris now, but will soon be slowly moving away from it in a wide circle that will bring it back to Polaris in about 26,000 years.

The greatest of the Hellenistic world's astronomers, the Alexandrian Ptolemy, believed that precession took place at a certain speed. To demonstrate this, he appears to have taken an old table of star positions and calculated the new positions based on his theory.[55] In fact, the stars were not where he calculated them to be. If he had made a new table of star positions by carefully looking at the locations of the stars in question he could have discovered his error and might have corrected it. When Muslim astronomers later calculated the rate correctly, they were misled into thinking that it had changed since Ptolemy's time. Ptolemy's error even confused Copernicus, who, comparing Ptolemy's figures with al-Battani's, wrote: "Hence it is also clear that the movement was least from the time of Aristarchus to that of Ptolemy and greatest from that of Ptolemy to al-Battani."[56] Kepler and Tycho Brahe even went along with the theory.[57] Yet, the fourteenth-century Muslim

---

[55] See Robert R. Newton, *Ancient Astronomical Observations and the Accelerations of the Earth and Moon*. Baltimore: Johns Hopkins University, 1970.

[56] Nicolaus Copernicus 1543, *On the Revolutions of the Heavenly Spheres*, translated by Charles Glenn Wallis, in *Great Books*, v. 16. Chicago: Encyclopaedia Britannica, Inc., 626. It is interesting that Copernicus states that he places "the utmost confidence" in al-Battani's observations, but regarding those of Hipparchus and Ptolemy he says only, "we have passed these things in review just as they were recorded by our predecessors" (624).

[57] Owen Gingerich, private communication (2003).

astronomer Ibn ash-Shatir demonstrated, observationally, that the theory that an earlier generation had devised to account for this nonexistent variation (called *trepidation*)[58] was not correct.[59] The theory was also rejected by Muhyi al-Din al-Mughribi[60] and al-Battani[61] and opposed by Tusi,[62] Sadr and Shirazi.[63] Muhyi al-Din al-Maghrabi (*d*. 1283) and Ibn al-Shatir's (*d*. 1375) calculated tropical longitudes based on constant precession and as a result their results are in better agreement with observations than tables from Andalus.[64]

The magnitude of Ptolemy's blunder has caused some modern scientists to accuse him of fraud.[64] In my view, he only took the

---

[58] The theory of trepidation goes back to Theon of Alexandria and was modifed by Thabit ibn Qurrah early in the Islamic era. By the time of ibn Shatir the baseline of accurate observations had become long enough to seriously question the entire theory on observational grounds.

[59] "The motion of trepidation [*ḥarakat al-Iqbāl wa-l-idbār*] is not sound because it contradicts what was found to be true in ancient and modern observations. In addition it is a false conception [*taṣawwur kādhib*]; this despite the fact that it would have been possible to imagine [*taṣawwur*] a setting of spheres that would produce this motion, provided that it existed in reality." Ibn ash-Shatir, *Nihāyat al-sūl fī tashīḥ al-uṣūl (The Final Quest Regarding the Rectification of [Astronomical] Principles)*, quoted by George Saliba in *A History of Arabic Astronomy: Planetary Theories During the Golden Age of Islam*. New York: NYU, 1994, 235.

[60] Jan P. Hogendijk and AbdelHamid I. Sabra, *The Enterprise of Science in Islam: New Perspectives*. Cambridge, MS: MIT Press, 2003, xvii.

[61] See George Sarton, *Introduction to History of Science I*, 446

[62] At-Tusi's measurements of precession in the 13th century gave the same value as al-Ma'mun's in the 4th century. Aydin Sayili, *The Observatory in Islam*. NY: Arno, 1981, 78.

[63] See Ahmad Salim Dallal, *The Astronomical Work of Sadr al-Shai'ah: An Islamic Response to Greek Astronomy*. Ann Arbor: University Microfilms International, 1990.

[64] Julio Samsó, "On the Lunar Tables in Sanjaq Dār Zīj al-Sharīf," in Hogendijk and Sabra, *The Enterprise of Science in Islam*, 286.

[65] Robert R. Newton, *The Crime of Claudius Ptolemy*. Baltimore: Johns Hopkins University, 1977. Actually, even at-Tusi seems to have hinted at a suspicion of fraud by predicting: "At a certain age, learned and *truthful* masters will ascertain the location of the stars, and a long time after, e.g., five hundred or one thousand years later, other masters will determine their positions anew, and it will thus become established how much each has moved during the interval separating the two sets of observations." Sayili, *Observatory*, 28.

prevailing attitude about the limited value of observation to science to an unfortunate extreme.[66] Remember the Greek view that astronomy is a branch of mathematics. A mathematician does not "look" to see if two plus two is four. Gingerich writes: "It is unfortunate that Ptolemy failed sometimes to distinguish between the theoretical and the observational, but that scarcely makes him a criminal."[67]

And how many Signs
In the heavens and the earth
Do they pass by? Yet they
Turn (their faces) away from them!

   – Qur'an (12:105)

Muslims took this warning seriously and devoted much effort and resources to the construction of major observatories. Nasr points out that the construction of these "observatories as distinct scientific institutions, in which observation is carried out, and also as centers for teaching astronomy and allied subjects, owes its origin to Islam."[68] Not only did Muslim rulers fund public observatories, but there were a number of private observatories as well.[68] 9Caliph Ma'mun, himself a scientist was especially generous reportedly paying on the order of 5,000 dinars per month to his best astronomers,[70] a sum that today would be associated with the salaries of professional athletes.

[66] Gingerich makes related arguments in detail. See Owen Gingerich, "Was Ptolemy a Fraud?" *Quarterly Journal Royal Astronomical Society* 21 (1980): 253. And Owen Gingerich, "Ptolemy Revisited: A Reply to R. R. Newton," *Quarterly Journal Royal Astronomical Society* 22 (1981): 40. Neither Newton nor Gingerich ever convinced the other. See Robert R Newton, *The Origins of Ptolemy's Astronomical Parameters*. (Baltimore: Johns Hopkins University, 1982, and Owen Gingerich, "The Origins of Ptolemy's Astronomical Parameters," (Review) *Journal History of Astronomy* 21 (1991): 364-65.

[67] Owen Gingerich, "Ptolemy Revisited," 22:40.

[68] Seyyed Hossein Nasr, *Science and Civilization in Islam*. 2nd ed. Cambridge UK: Islamic Texts Society, 1987, 80.

[69] Sayili, *Observatory*, 90-95.

[69] Sayili, *Observatory*, 92.

The earliest Muslims were not scientists. At first, Islamic science, as all science does, had to build on the work of the past. Yet, we shall show in the Chapter 5 that the Muslims were able to move beyond the heritage from ancient Greece, not only in terms of their scientific progress but also in qualitative terms. They moved into what is, in essence, modern science.

What placed Muslims in this advantageous position in the pursuit of science? Certainly, religious problems often entailed astronomical solutions (e.g., calculating the dates of holy days,[71] the times of prayer, and the direction of prayer, the *qibla*). This explains why the Islamic tradition involved a unique research into the times of dawn and twilight, including a proposed explanation for the false dawn," a phenomenon not even known to Europeans until centuries later.[72] The reliance of religious ritual on astronomical information cannot be the complete answer, however, as other civilizations had to contend with similar questions. Medieval Christianity needed to set the date of Easter, for example. This unavoidable religious requirement[73] did not spur the European Christians into an explosion of scientific progress. Besides, scientific information needed for religious rituals could be met without the extraordinary efforts that went into the Muslim observatories.[74]

---

[71] For a detailed discussion of the calendar issues, see Chapter 7.

[72] Dallal, *Astronomical Work of Sadr*, 454.

[73] The ecclesiastical rule initiated by Constantine in the fourth century only gradually took hold. Easter would be the first Sunday after the full moon after the vernal equinox. This rule involved no astronomical calculation of the vernal equinox, but simply defined the vernal equinox as March 21. Even the full moon itself was neither observed nor properly calculated, but simply defined as the fourteenth day after the new moon. In the Eighth century, Bede documented that a different rule was used by the Irish church as late as the sixth century and the dispute between the Irish and the Roman Church was resolved by political rather than astronomical adjudication. The Eastern and Roman churches still observe Easter on different days.

[74] Sayili, *Observatory*, 130.

I believe that the following factors, some of which did not play a significant role in earlier scientific cultures, were conducive to scientific progress in the Islamic civilization: (1) the Qur'anic mandate to observe nature; (2) the universality of Islam, which provides a hospitable environment for the universality favorable to scientific progress; (3) the prohibition of a priesthood; (4) the acceptability of material prosperity; (5) the requirement of freedom of thought; (6) the development of careful citation in hadith science; (7) the Qur'anic emphasis on learning and study. Consider how each of these factors made Islamic and the scientific traditions that followed it different in a manner that we might consider modern:

(1) The Qur'anic mandate to observe nature spurs us towards the scientific method of induction.

> Say: "Behold all that is
> In the heavens and on earth;"
> But neither Signs nor Warners
> Profit those who believe not.
>> – Qur'an (10:101)

> If there were, in the heavens
> And the earth, other gods
> Besides God, there would
> Have been confusion in both!
>> – Qur'an (21:22)

The contrast between the Islamic view of a nature packed with the signs of God that we are commanded to observe with the Platonic distrust of the senses is unmistakable. Muhammad Iqbal has emphasized

> the general empirical attitude of the Qur'an which engendered in its followers a feeling of reverence for the actual, and ultimately made them the founders of modern science.

It was a great point to awaken the empirical spirit in an age that renounced the visible as of no value in men's search after God.[75]

The Qur'an does not see empirical observation, rational thought, and gnostic contemplation as pulling men in different directions. It insists that all lead to God. Thus, we are repeatedly exhorted to "see,"[76] to "think,"[77] and to "contemplate."[78]

(2) As Islam spread, its universality prevented the Arabs from a crippling disdain for the scientific knowledge of the Greeks, Persians, Indians, Chinese, etc. All good comes from God. This open-minded embrace of knowledge from any source is reflected in the Islamic proverb advising the Muslims to "seek knowledge even unto China."[79] One exemplary case of how the Prophet himself applied this principle was when he ditched his own plans for the defense of Medina in order to adopt a plan to dig a trench around the city, put forward by Salman-al-Farsi. This was a technique that the Persian Salman had picked up in his homeland and was hitherto unknown in Arabia. The Prophet judged the suggestion by its merits, not by the nationality of the proposer. This objectivity about the sources of knowledge is, of course, merely an extension of Islam's more general principle of brotherhood:

---

[75] Muhammad Iqbal, 1944. *The Reconstruction of Religious Thought in Islam.* www.yespakistan.com/iqbal/reconstruction/1-4.95p(accessed 2/4/06).

[76] "Say: See ye? If God were to make the Day perpetual over you to the Day of Judgment, what god is there other than God, Who can give you a Night in which ye can rest? Will ye not then see?"– Qur'an 28:72.

[77] "Now let man but think from what he is created!" – Qur'an 86:5.

[78] "... contemplate the (wonders of) creation in the heavens and the earth, (with the thought): 'Our Lord! not for naught hast Thou created (all) this!'" – Qur'an 3:191.

[79] Muhammad Azizullah, *Glimpses of the Hadith.* Takoma Park, MD: Crescent Publications, 1972. Although this proverb is often misquoted as a hadith, it may have been inspired by the hadith quoted in the Sunan of Abu-Dawood (#1631), "If anyone travels on a road in search of knowledge, God will cause him to travel on one of the roads of Paradise."

O mankind! We created
You from a single (pair)
Of a male and a female,
And made you into
Nations and tribes, that
Ye may know each other
(Not that ye may despise
Each Other).
> – Qur'an (49:13)

The expanding Muslim civilization was "the first to give science the international character which we consider one of its fundamental characteristics."[80]

(3) The abolition of the priesthood and prohibitions of secrecy prevented scientific knowledge from becoming the property of an elite. Knowledge was available to everyone. In the Christian world, people went to the church for religious instruction only. Even that instruction was a "lay" instruction, fit for the layman. Reading of the Bible itself was discouraged for those not initiated into the priesthood. The subtle doctrines of Christian theology might confuse the layman and weaken his faith. It was better to provide him with pre-digested teaching.

By contrast every Muslim was expected to read and preferably memorize the Qur'an, opening the door to universal literacy.[81] (The very first word of the Qur'an revealed to Muhammad was the commandment "Read!") All knowledge was considered sacred and people came to the mosque to study not only the Qur'an and the traditions, but mathematics, history, natural science, etc. As

---

[80] René Taton, *Ancient and Modern Science From the Beginning to 1450*. New York: Basic Books, 1963.

[81] Marshall G. S. Hodgson, *The Venture of Islam: Conscience and History in a World Civilization 2: The Expansion of Islam in the Middle Periods*. Chicago: University of Chicago Press, 1961, 118.

the numbers of teachers and classes exceeded the space in the mosque, additional buildings would be added around it. Thus, the world came to know its first modern universities.

Terms coined in that era are still in use today. The teachers would sit in low chairs with the students gathered on the carpeted floor around them. A new student interested in learning, say mathematics, could walk into the mosque and ask, "Where is the chair of mathematics?" or "Where is the chair of astronomy?"

The desire of Muslims to bring knowledge to the general public can be seen in the title of Anu'l-Wafa al-Buzjani's *Book on the Settling What Is Necessary from the Science of Arithmetic for Secretaries and Businessmen* (written in the late tenth century) and in Abu Bakr Muhammad al-Karaji's description of his book *Sufficient Arithmetic* (written in the early 11th century) as one that "presents what people of different classes need for their various activities."[82] Al-Khwarithmi did not conceive of his famous book on algebra (see p. 73) as a theoretical work, but as a practical work for a broad target audience, "to provide 'what is easiest is most useful in arithmetic, such as men constantly require in cases of inheritance, legacies, partition, lawsuits, and trade, and in all their dealings with one another, or where the measuring of lands, the digging of canals, geometrical computations, and other objects of various sorts and kinds are concerned.'"[83]

(4) A materially successful society can afford to support pure science. Other previous societies that had enjoyed some degree of prosperity had also supported science. The prosperity under Islam, however, was *unprecedented*, especially given the way it was spread throughout almost all layers of society. Before Islamic civilization had reached its second century, patronage of the arts and sciences had reached new heights.

---

[82] Yvonne Dold-Simplonius, "Calculating Surface Areas and Volumes in Islamic Architecture," in Hogendijk and Sabra, *Enterprise of Science in Islam*, 235-265.

[83] See previous note.

(5) Academic freedom, necessary for science to move forward, was inherent in the Islamic idea of individual responsibility. The Qur'an advises man that God is "nearer to him than (his) jugular vein" (50:16), that "no bearer of burdens can bear the burdens of another" (53:38), and "Whoever works any act of righteousness and has faith,–his endeavor will not be rejected: We shall record it in his favor" (21:94). As everyone is directly responsible to the Creator, and the priesthood is abolished, disputes are to be resolved not by human authority but by truth–whatever God may have decreed it to be.

We shall show later that Church interference into scientific matters was based on what was perceived to be a threat to the religion. In Islam, even matters of religion are not exempt from frank and honest discussion. Consider this excerpt from a letter of Hashimi, a cousin of the Caliph Ma'mun, to a religious opponent:

> ... bring forward all the arguments you wish and say whatever you please and speak your mind freely. Now that you are safe and free to say whatever you please appoint some arbitrator who will impartially judge between us and lean only towards the truth and be free from the empery of passion, and that arbitrator shall be Reason, whereby God makes us responsible for our own rewards and punishments. Herein I have dealt justly with you and have given you full security and am ready to accept whatever decision Reason may give for me or against me. For "There is no compulsion in religion" (Qur'an 2:256) and I have only invited you to accept our faith willingly and of your own accord and have pointed out the hideousness of your present belief. Peace be with you and the blessings of God![84]

---

[84] Thomas Walker Arnold 1913, *The Preaching of Islam: A History of the Propagation of the Muslim Faith*. Lahore: Ashraf, 1961, 144.

As the Middle Ages drew to a close, the Church identified this attitude as an Islamic one and actively sought to combat its persistence in the regions recently reconquered. Thus, in 1602, among the charges brought up in the Spanish Inquisition against the "Apostacies and Treasons of the Moriscoes" was "that they commended nothing so much as that liberty of conscience in all matters of religion, which the Turks, and all other Mohammedans, suffer their subjects to enjoy."[85]

(6) The natural sciences in Islam had a model in the development of the religious sciences as to proper citation and investigation of the credibility of sources. The early Muslims, like the early Christians, had to contend with a plethora of "traditions" attributed to the religion's founder. The Christians relied on the authority of a central Church (backed by the state) to resolve the issue. Having no priesthood, the Muslim scholars invented new techniques of historical scholarship.

Scholars such as Imams Bukhari and Muslim went on long expeditions to track down traditions (called hadith) attributed to the Prophet's companions to their sources. They determined the complete chain of transmission from the Prophet's companion to the particular reporter whom they were able to find. They made biographies of every transmitter in the chain to determine their reliability for honesty, soundness of memory, plausibility of having met adjacent members in the chain of transmission, etc. Thus, Muslim historians became accustomed to the process of *citation*, something that is an indispensable part of modern science. The vagueness of ancient historians about their sources stands in stark contrast to the insistence that scholars such as Bukhari and Muslim manifested in knowing every member in a chain of transmission and examining their reliability. They published their findings,

---

[85] See J. Morgan, *Mohametism Explained* (London, 1723-1725), II, 297-8, 345.

which were then subjected to additional scrutiny by future scholars for consistency with each other and the Qur'an. By the third century of Islam this methodology was well developed.

Such open "historical criticism" of the Islamic traditions is a process to which Christian texts have been subjected only in recent centuries. It is a process of analysis and preservation in the form of a *scientific* study. Hadith science was original with Islam. It was the first uniquely Islamic science and provided a precedent for open and rigorous scholarly debate in the natural sciences that were being assimilated into the emerging Islamic culture. This precedent of reasonable *questioning* of authority accords citation the kind of critical respect it enjoys in the sciences rather than the blind adherence frequently associated with religion.

(7) From the very first word of the Qur'an revealed (*Iqra!*, which means "Read!"), praising the "Lord who taught man by the pen," the Qur'an (96:1) emphasizes learning and study in all its aspects. Qur'anic teachings on the importance of knowledge to religion and the pointing out of the signs of God in the heavens and on earth provided an incentive for the patronage of science.

> Behold! In the creation
> Of the heavens and the earth;
> In the alternation
> Of the Night and the Day;
> In the sailing of the ships
> Through the Ocean
> For the profit of mankind;
> In the rain which God
> Sends down from the skies,
> And the life which
> He gives therewith
> To an earth that is dead;
> In the beasts of all kinds

That He scatters
Through the earth;
In the change of the winds,
And the clouds which they
Trail like their slaves
Between the sky and the earth;–
(Here) indeed are Signs
For a people that are wise.

     – Qur'an (2:164)

Here is a small sampling of the numerous references to signs in the sky.

Do not the Unbelievers see
That the heavens and the earth
Were joined together (as one
Unit of Creation), before
We clove them asunder?
We made from water
Every living thing. Will they
Not then believe?

     – Qur'an (21:30)

Moreover He comprehended
In His design the sky,
And it had been (as) smoke:
He said to it
And to the earth:
"Come ye together,
Willingly or unwillingly."
They said: "We do come
(Together), in willing obedience."

     – Qur'an (41:11)

God is He Who
Created seven Firmaments
And of the earth
A similar number.
Through the midst
Of them (all) descends His
Command: that ye may
Know that God has power
Over all things, and that
God comprehends all things
In (His) Knowledge.

        – Qur'an (65:12)

It is He Who created
The Night and the Day,
And the sun and the moon:
All (the celestial bodies)
Swim along, each in its
Rounded course.

        – Qur'an (21:33)

The Qur'an lays stress on understanding and on observing the signs in heaven and earth. It emphasizes the harmony between the observation of these signs and the universality of God's laws (evidence of His existence and His compassion). The religious requirement for empirical study and for faith in the harmony of such research with rational analysis leads directly to the scientific method in which experiment and observation are checks on theory, and *vice versa*.

In the succeeding chapters we shall examine how Islamic science evolved. We shall start with a review of three astronomical events reported by the Prophet's own companions. Recalling that they were a people "who neither write nor count," we shall observe that while the Prophet offered no scientific theories for the breath-taking spectacles reported, he did insist that they were without superstitious significance. Rather, they were signs of God, and subsequently of His sovereignty over all things. We shall then show how the Islamic unified perspective (*tawhīd*) interacted with the various scientific heritages of Greece, Persia, India, etc., with which it made contact. We shall see that although Greek rationalism or Christian gnosticism had an influence on various Muslim scientists, Muslim science was most purely Islamic when it was most inductive; and that the scientists who were most inductive are the ones whose significance is least understood in the West. Finally, we shall look at the impact of Islamic science on modern science. Although the most Hellenized (Greek-influenced) of the Islamic scientists are the best known, it is scientists such as al-Biruni who were most true to the Islamic spirit, who were most innovative, and whose impact, while less direct, was most profound.

Figure 3
Total Solar Eclipse of 1970 (NASA)

He merges Night into Day,
And He merges Day into Night,
And He has subjected the sun and the moon (to His Law):
Each one runs its course for a term appointed.
– Qur'an (35:6)

CHAPTER 4

WHAT MUHAMMAD SAW IN THE SKY

Just as it is not a condition of religion to reject medical science, so likewise the rejection of natural science is not one of its conditions, except ... [that religion requires] the recognition that nature is entirely subject to God; incapable of acting by itself, it is an instrument in the hand of the Creator. Sun, moon, stars, and elements are subject to His command. – *al-Ghazali* [86]

Before Islam, the Arabs were an unlettered and superstitious people. With cause, Muslims refer to the pre-Islamic period as the Age of Ignorance (al-jāhilīya). The pre-Islamic Arabs associated the planetary bodies with pagan gods and goddesses. To them, eclipses were signs of events in human affairs.

The Islamic scientific civilization, despite its rapid appearance and growth, did not spring up overnight. The Prophet remained illiterate to his death. He knew nothing about science.[87] Yet, though he had no scientific knowledge, skills or training, he had a scientific attitude. Before we plunge into the history of astronomy and astronomical science itself, let us take a look at three events reported in the hadith to see what light they shed on the Prophet's attitude.

---

[86] *The Deliverance from Error* in W. Montgomery Watt, trans., *The Faith and Practice of Al-Ghazzali*. Liverpool: Tinling, 1953. Also:
http://www.muslimphilosophy.com/gz/works/watt3.htm (accessed 10/28/03).

[87] The Qur'an's remarkable durability in the face of the changes in scientific currents and the occurrence of major revolutions in scientific thought cannot be attributed to scientific insight on the part of the Prophet. Maurice Buccaille (see Maurice Buccaille, *The Bible, Qur'an and Science*. Paris: Seghers, 1981) has written a fascinating book arguing that it reflects the divine origin of that Book, instead. While some of his statements on astronomy are open to question, I found his observations on biology and physiology (Buccaille is a physician) compelling. However, his work has inspired a wave of Muslim pseudoscience, discussed in Chapter 8 of this work.

I will relate three incidents in the life of the Prophet that may be related to the observation of celestial events: *Lailat-ul-qadr* (the "Night of Measure" on which the Qur'an was first revealed), *inshaqat-al-qamr* (the "splitting" of the moon), and an eclipse of the sun. All the data that I report come from the most respected of collections of the Prophetic traditions (hadith, see Chapter 3), the Sahīh Bukhāri and the *Sahīh Muslim*.[88] I find in these reports an indication that the Prophet's attitude towards stunning astronomical sights was free from superstition. Rather than seeking omens about mundane human affairs, he saw in every case a sign of God's greatness and an opportunity to reflect on humanity's ultimate destiny.

Lailat-ul-qadr
(The Night of Measure)[89]

Lailat-ul-qadr (Arabic for the Night of Power, or the Night of Measure) is the name for the night on which the first revelation to the Prophet Muhammad (peace be upon him) took place. The exact date of this event is uncertain.

Lailat-ul-qadr took place while the Prophet was engaged in the practice of *i'tikāf*–seclusion for prayer and fasting. The Qur'an says "The Night of Power is better than a thousand months" (Qur'an 97:3). Muslims understand that the blessings derived from this one night's prayers and meditation exceed those of a thousand months of devotions. They observe an all-night vigil in emulation of the Prophet. They desire to perform these devotions on the same night of the year as Muhammad's initial revelation. This is what is meant

---

[88] Despite the great care that those authors took in compiling their collections, we must always remember that what they produced are historical reports of the Prophet's life compiled centuries after his death. Notwithstanding the exalted character of the figure at their center, they are subject to similar doubts and uncertainties as any other historical reports.

[89] The following is based on a talk given to the American Astronomical Society Historical Division, Imad A. Ahmad, "The Dawn Sky on *Lailat-ul-qadr* (the Night of Power)." *Bulletin of the American Astronomical Society,* 21 (1989): 1217.

by the Prophet's instructions on how to "seek" *Lailat-ul-qadr*, as in the following, taken from the *Sahīh Muslim*:

> ... I started devoting myself in the last ten (nights [of Ramadan]). And he who desires to observe *i'tikāf* along with me should spend the (night) at his place of *i'tikāf*. And I saw this night (*Lailat-ul-qadr*) but I forgot it (the exact night); so seek it in the last ten nights on odd numbers.[90]

The hadith is clear that it was on an odd-numbered day during the last ten days of the month of Ramadan in the Julian year 610.[91] Some astronomers have made computer calculations as to what the sky looked like on that marvelous night.

When two objects in the sky come very close to one another, at the same celestial longitude, astronomers say there is a "conjunction" of the two bodies.[92] Gerald Hawkins (famous for his work on Stonehenge) found that a conjunction of the moon and Venus took place in the dawn sky of July 23, 610. He noted that the precise configuration matches a commonly used symbol of Islam, the star and crescent. Hawkins' observation is very interesting. The horns of the moon in the famous Islamic symbol are reversed from the more commonly seen lunar crescent symbol. They point to the right and not to the left. The horns of a new moon point to the left. It seems that the horns in the star and crescent symbol must be the *old* moon, the one near the end of a month. This would be an appropriate symbol for *Lailat-ul-qadr*, which took place near the *end* of Ramadan.

---

[90] Abdul Hamid Siddiqi, *Sahīh Muslim*. Lahore: Ashraf, 1976 , ch. 441 #2625.

[91] Ramadan is the ninth month of the Islamic lunar calendar. The Ramadan in which *Lailat-ul-qadr* took place fell in the period of June-July 610 C.E. On the Islamic calendar, dates begin at sunset before the corresponding date on the common era calendar and end at the next day's sunset.

[92] The positions of objects in the sky are indicated by latitude and longitude just as are the positions of places on earth. Celestial longitude is simply the lines of longitude on the earth's surface projected onto the sky. Thus, a star that is directly above 75° West longitude at a given time is said to be a 75° West longitude in the sky.

On the other hand, it has often been claimed that the star and crescent symbol we now know of did not acquire its association with Islam until the late Ottoman era. Further, Schaefer has reported that the star and crescent symbol antedates the Islamic era. He states that an Arab-Sassanian coin from 651 C.E. bearing the star and crescent symbol "is virtually an identical copy of a pre-Islamic Sassanian coin."[93]

Did this conjunction really happen on *Lailat-ul-qadr*? The Islamic calendar is a strict lunar calendar. Every twelve months (orbits of the moon around the earth with respect to the sun) makes one year. Thus, it only requires counting lunar cycles to calculate in which month the conjunction of the moon and Venus took place. It was indeed in the month of Ramadan. It was certainly on the 25th, 26th or 27th. Unfortunately, to decide on which of these dates it occurred is somewhat complicated.

Whichever of these dates it may have been, it was definitely during Muhammad's *i'tikāf*, the period of fasting and meditation which he spent in the cave of Mt. Hirah. It is very likely, then, that he saw this inspiring sight on the pre-dawn sky on or near *Lailat-ul-qadr*.

Although Hawkins was correct about the month in which this conjunction took place, it seems doubtful that it was the 27th of Ramadan. In Chapter 7, we shall explain in detail the Islamic calendar, which is based on sighting the new moon. For now, it is enough to understand that the new moon as understood by astronomers (that is, the conjunction of the moon with the sun, when the moon crosses from being west of the sun to being east of the sun) cannot be seen by humans on earth. (See Chapter 7 for details.) The practice of the Prophet, however, was to determine the new month by an actual sighting. As Hawkins notes, the astronomical new moon took place on June 26. However, his estimate of the date of sighting (June 26 or 27) is impossible. Because of the many factors that prevent the new moon from being sighted as a visible crescent until many hours after new moon, the new crescent sighting must have been on June 27 or 28.

One might ask if Muhammad dated his report of *Lailat-ul-qadr* from a false crescent sighting on June 26. The meticulous care with which Muhammad cited his uncertainty about the date in the excerpt quoted above from the *Sahīh Muslim* argues against this.

The traditions vary about the precise night, but all are consistent that it was an odd-numbered night. This means that despite his uncertainty over the exact date, Muhammad was certain that the date was an odd number. Such certainty is meaningless unless he was also certain about what date was the first of Ramadan.

Based on the preceding, I conclude that the conjunction took place on either the 26th or 25th of Ramadan. If on the 26th, then the date, being an even number, fails to satisfy the requirement that *Lailat-ul-qadr* fall on an odd-numbered night. If on the 25th, then it suggests that either the 25th is *Lailat-ul-qadr* (and not the 27th as most commonly practiced by the Muslim community) or else the conjunction did not take place on *Lailat-ul-qadr*.

Is it just a coincidence that the star and crescent matches the conjunction of July 23rd? There are no coincidences. In Allah's hands are all things. Then what is the meaning of the symbolism?

The pre-Islamic Arabs associated Venus, the moon and the sun with the goddesses al-Uzza, al-Lat and Manat. The three goddesses are named in the same surah that describes the revelation of *Lailat-ul-qadr*: "These are nothing but names which ye have devised—ye and your fathers, for which God has sent down no authority (whatever)" Qur'an (53:23). This is consistent with an interpretation that there are no animate beings corresponding to the three bodies rising over Mecca in the dawn of July 23, 610.

Remember that the idea that contemplation of the "signs in the heavens and the earth" as leading to the conclusion of the existence of a single God is a recurrent theme in the Qur'an. In Chapter 2, we recounted Abraham's experience of arriving at monotheism through astronomical observations of celestial objects worshiped as deities. The Qur'anic passage relates his study and rejection as objects of worship: a star [kawkab], the moon, and the sun, in that order (Qur'an 6:75-78).

Buccaille has argued in *The Bible, the Qur'an and Science* that the word *kawkab* should be translated as "planet" rather than "star."[94] If we assume that *kawkab* here refers to Venus, the star and crescent becomes a symbol of the parallel between the missions of Abraham and Muhammad (peace be upon them both). It is fascinating that the three bodies are sighted by Abraham in the same order that they rose over Mecca on July 23, 610–and in the same order that the goddesses associated with them are mentioned in the Qur'anic quotation given in Chapter 2. Before that, there seems to be no reference to the star and crescent in the hadith.

Hawkins suggested that the star and crescent "might be a product of the collective subconscious of what was seen on the 'Night of Power.'" There is another possible explanation. Perhaps a Muslim astrologer,[95] long after Muhammad, may have sought to know what the astrological configuration was at the time of *Lailat-ul-qadr*. This supposed astrologer may have counted forward 27 days from the astronomical new moon (being unaware that the astronomical new moon cannot be seen) and concluded that there was a conjunction of the moon and Venus on the 27th of Ramadan. His now forgotten horoscope might have been the origin of the symbol. This is mere speculation, but so is Hawkins' hypothesis.

---

[94] See Buccaille, *The Bible*.

[95] Despite Islam's opposition to divinatory astrology, it was nonetheless popular, just as it is popular today in the West despite hostility both from modern astronomers and Christian teaching.

Our explanation, at least, has the advantage of explaining the apparent lack of association between the symbol and Islam before the Ottoman era. A pre-existing Turkish symbol may have been adopted by Muslims under the Ottomans. The hypothetical astrologer seeking the date of *Lailat-ul-qadr* might have mistaken July 23 as the 27th of Ramadan. Many Muslim countries make such a one-day error today in setting their calendars, being unaware that the new crescent cannot be seen until many hours after the conjunction of the sun and the moon (see Chapter 7).

Perhaps the conjunction of Venus and the moon served as a source of inspiration for the Prophet. Or, perhaps the star and crescent is merely the result of a later-date Muslim's efforts at astrology. We must not be dogmatic in arriving at astronomical conclusions from mythological, literary, and religious sources. Otherwise, we risk falling into that class of people the Qur'an warns against: "They follow nothing but conjecture and what their own souls desire..." (53:23).

Inshaq-al-qamar
(The Splitting of the Moon)[96]

Of all the hadith touching on astronomical bodies, there is none as difficult as those relating the Prophet's observation, in the company of some believers and some pagans at Mina, of the "splitting of the moon." The following eyewitness description of the event, as reported by 'Abdullah Ibn Mas'ud, is taken from the *Sahih Muslim*:

We were along with God's Messenger (peace be upon him) at Mina when the moon was split in two. One of its parts was beyond the mountain and the other one was on this side of it. God's messenger (peace be upon him) said to us: "Witness."[97]

---

[96] The following is based on a talk given to the American Astronomical Society, Imad A. Ahmad, "Did Muhammad Witness a Canterbury Swarm?" *Bulletin of the American Astronomical Society,* 19 (1988): 1011.

[97] Imad A. Ahmad, "Did Muhammad Witness? 1011.

The provocative phrase "the moon was split in two" has caused some Muslims to believe that the moon was physically split into two separated parts. I shall show that an alternative explanation is much more likely. The greater likelihood of my proposed explanation is not based on the principles of natural science alone. The claim that the Prophet and his companions witnessed a miracle of the scale implied by the physical splitting of the moon runs into difficulty from a Qur'anic standpoint. Here is the argument the Qur'an provided to the Prophet against those who demanded miracles:

And thou wast not (able)
To recite a Book before
This (Book came), nor art thou
(Able) to transcribe it
With thy right hand:
In that case, indeed, would
The talkers of vanities
Have doubted.

Nay, here are Signs
Self-evident in the hearts
Of those endowed with knowledge:
And none but the unjust
Reject Our Signs.

Yet they say:
"Why are not Signs sent down
To him from his Lord?"
Say: "The Signs are indeed
With God: and I am
Indeed a clear Warner."

And is it not enough
For them that We have
Sent down to thee
The Book which is rehearsed
To them? Verily, in it
Is Mercy and a Reminder
To those who believe.

Say: "Enough is God
For a Witness between me
And you: He knows
What is in the heavens
And on earth. And it is
Those who believe in vanities
And reject God, that
Will perish (in the end)."
                    – Qur'an (29:48-52)

Clearly the Qur'an itself is the Prophet's miracle.

The astute reader will notice that the issue of whether anyone is entitled to make dogma of a particular interpretation of a hadith ties into the main point of my thesis. In Chapter 2, I accused the Medieval Christians of hostility to unrestrained scientific inquiry because of its potential threat to Church dogma, and I will return to that theme in Chapter 6. My thesis is that Islam was, in the golden era, relatively free of such impediments. The desire of some modern Muslims to wield dogma as a club against intellectual inquiry in no way reflects the classical Islamic attitudes and it certainly is opposed to the Qur'an.

The last two words in a celebrated line from the Qur'an in a chapter called "The Moon" (al-qamar), are inshaq-al-qamar. Yusuf Ali renders this in English as "The moon is cleft asunder."

A literal translation would be "The moon (is) split in two." The scholars of Islam provided three principal interpretations of this verse. Either it is (1) an allegorical statement, (2) a prophetic reference to the last days, or (3) a reference to an actual phenomenon observed by some residents of Mecca, including the Prophet, some of his companions, and some polytheists.

Those who favor the last interpretation should know that some English monks used the same words to describe an event that they witnessed from Canterbury in the twelfth century. Brecher writes that the monks reported that just after sunset on June 25, 1178 (on the Gregorian calendar) "the upper horn of the new moon seemed split in two and a flame shot from it."[98] Brecher interpreted this description as evidence for a swarm of meteoroids associated with Comet Encke, one of which struck the moon creating the observed effect. He dubbed the meteoroids "the Canterbury swarm" and argued that it is the same swarm that has been associated with both the famous Stony Tunguska River explosion that rocked Siberia on June 30, 1908 and the five-day rain of meteoroids detected by Apollo mission instruments on the moon's surface in 1975 (June 22-26).

Was God trying to indicate the presence of a prophet among the English monks? It seems more likely that neither event was miraculous and that the phenomenon seen by the Prophet and his companions is also related to the Canterbury swarm. This seems especially likely when we notice that *surat-at-tāriq* (the 86th surah of the Qur'an) was revealed at about the same time as *al-qamar* (the 54th surah of the Qur'an).[99] The former describes "the night visitant" (*at-tāriq*) as *an-najmuth-thāqib,* a star of piercing brightness. The

---

[98] K. Brecher, *Bulletin of the American Astronomical Society.* 16 (1984): 476.

[99] The major divisions of the Qur'an are into units each of which is called a *surah*. These are not numbered chronologically, but rather in the order that the Prophet recited them when he recited the entire Qur'an.

hypothesis that a "splitting of the moon" may be caused by a meteor swarm associated with a comet suggests that this visiting star might also be interpreted as a reference to a comet.

My own research has shown that the most likely Gregorian calendar date for the phenomenon seen by the Prophet and his companions at Mina is either May 26-27 or June 26-27.[100] The latter date is perfectly consistent with the hypothesis that the same swarm of meteoroids caused both of the "moon splittings."

It is interesting that the moon was approximately full on this date. Thus, it would have been on the horizon in the early evening, the most likely time of night for an encounter between the two antagonistic groups–Muslims and polytheists–to be looking at the moon together. The description quoted on page 55 suggests that the moon was near the horizon. The fact that the moon was full would explain the one striking difference in the descriptions between the Mina and Canterbury events. In the Canterbury observation, it is reported that a bright plume ("a flame") shot from the moon. On Brecher's interpretation, this was relatively bright ejected matter seen against the dark surface of the new moon. Such ejecta would not appear as a "flame" when the moon was full. If seen at all, it would appear dark.

Although the association of the Mina event with the Canterbury swarm seems consistent, caution is still called for. The reference to a mountain between the two parts of the moon is troubling. Could the reference merely be to a mountain peak dividing the moon into two parts? This is not likely since the hadithic reports refer to the phenomenon as an "ayat," or sign, of God. Such a term is usually applied to more spectacular events such as eclipses. If, on the other hand, the reference to the mountain is taken as an indication of a physical separation between the two "parts" of the moon (a view

---

[100] Imad A. Ahmad, "Did Muhammad Witness a Canterbury Swarm?" *Bulletin of the American Astronomical Society*, 19 (1988): 101 f.

adhered to by those contemporary Muslims who believe that the reported phenomenon was a physical miracle), then the possibility that the phenomenon was an illusion caused by the earth's atmosphere must be addressed.

Such a view was held by the classical Islamic astronomer Ibn `Ashshur who suggested that a second image of the moon may have been manifested in the sky not unlike the secondary image of the sun we call a sun-dog. Ibn`Ashshur's argument was based on the fact that the event was reported only at Mina and not elsewhere.[101] If we believe that the Mina event has an atmospheric explanation, then so may the Canterbury event–which also appears to have gone undetected elsewhere. This is not quite as surprising in the latter case, however, since the moon was new and the event could have only been seen along a narrow band on the earth's surface in any case.

On the other hand, the reference may be to a "mountain" of dark ejecta on the moon itself. God knows best.

The Eclipse of the Sun[102]

The Muslims of Medina saw an eclipse of the sun on the day that the Prophet's infant son, Ibrahim, died. In a paper I delivered to the American Astronomical Society, I showed that the hadithic reports of this eclipse are consistent with modern astronomers' theories of the slowing down of the earth's rotation.

The moon goes around the earth once every 29-1/2 days. Thus, it must pass between the earth and sun once in each orbit. Sometimes it passes exactly in front of the sun causing an eclipse as the solid body of the moon blots out the sun's light. The sky

---

[101] Taha Jabir Alalwani, private communication 1992.

[102] The following is based on a talk given to the American Astronomical Society Historical Division, Imad A. Ahmad, *A Uniform Islamic Calendar for the Western Hemisphere. (411 A.H.-1413 A.H.).* Bethesda: Imad-ad-Dean, Inc., 1990.

darkens. The temperature drops. In the moments before the last rays of the sun are blocked out, bands of shadows, alternating light and dark, race across the surface of the earth. The lunar valleys through which the sun's final rays shine as totality approaches look like a string of bright beads. The last glimpse of the brilliant surface of the sun looks like a diamond set in a ring of the sun's inner atmosphere. As the eclipse becomes total, birds stop singing and night-dwelling insects begin to chirp. The black disk of the moon is surrounded by the faint outer atmosphere of the sun, now visible to the naked eye. A kind of hairy crown, it is called the corona. Its shape traces the magnetic field of the sun. After a few minutes the process reverses itself. It is one of the most awe-inspiring sights seen by the eye of man.

To primitive people such as the pre-Islamic Arabs such an event was the cause of great fear. Muhammad, however, showed his people how to overcome this fear. He cut short a journey or ride somewhere upon realizing the eclipse was taking place to return in forenoon and lead them in prayer. He prayed aloud. A second recitation was made after first bow in each of the two *raka‘ā*.[103] The first *qiyām*[104] was almost the length of *sūrat-al-baqara* (the longest surah in the Qur'an) and subsequent *qiyāms* were long yet shorter than the first. His bowing and prostration were extremely extended, more so in the first than second *rakāh*. A woman fainted from the duration of the eclipse prayer and others found the length trying. By the end of prayer, the sun had cleared. A late-comer saw only two surahs and two *raka‘ā*, both recited after the late-comer perceived the eclipse to have ended.[105]

---

[103] The prayer is divided into segments called *raka‘āt*, (singular: *rak‘ah*) each of which ends with a pair of prostrations.

[104] The part of the prayer in which the worshiper is standing.

[105] These facts are collected from *Sahīh Bukhārī*, 1:86, 2:150-172 and 7:125, 8:219 and *Sahīh Muslim*, 1966-1991.

When some of the people said that the sun had eclipsed because of the death of Muhammad's infant son Ibrahim, the Prophet quickly corrected them. "The sun and moon are signs of God," he said "and do not eclipse for the death or birth of any man."[106]

This wonderful story demonstrates the modernity of the Prophet's attitude towards astronomical science, despite his lack of knowledge of the subject. He in no way confused the divine mysteries suggested by the awesomeness of astronomical phenomena with the superstition of his contemporaries. Thus, the sun and moon are signs reminding us of God and not the omens of mundane affairs as the astrologers would have it.

Despite the popularity of astrology throughout the Islamic era (and in our own in the West),[107] it is clearly not Islamic in its premises. The blurry line between astrology and astronomy was a source of annoyance to al-Ghazali who denounced it by appealing to words he attributed to the Prophet and his companions as well as by logical argument:

> The Prophet said: I fear three things for my followers after me, the oppression of the leaders, faith in Astrology, and disbelief in Taqdir (predecree). Hazrat Omar said: "Learn Astrology to conduct you in land and sea and not more."
> ...[Astrology] is harmful for the majority of people, because thoughts occur in their minds that it is the stars which influence the course of events and so the stars are to be worshiped. The wise man knows that the sun and the moon and

---

[106] Muhammad H. Haykal, *The Life of Muhammad*. North American Trust, 1976. See *Sahīh Bukhārī*, 2:153, 168, 170.

[107] The great science fiction writer Robert Heinlein ruefully pointed out that at any major magazine store you can find half dozen astrology magazines, but would be fortunate to find even one astronomy magazine.

the stars are subject to the command of God. The second reason is that Astrology is purely guesswork.[108]

I have related these three incidents because, apart from the inherently interesting astronomical and religious issues they raise, they demonstrate a certain attitude on the part of the Prophet. Like Abraham, he understood that behind the spectacle that these events provided was a lesson about the Designer behind the phenomena. We shall now turn to review the work of the scientists of the succeeding centuries of Islamic civilization and their attempts to discern the details of the grand scheme behind the signs in the heavens.

---

[108] al-Ghazali, *Ihya*. vol. 1, 47-48. Ibn Khaldun in his *Muqaddamah* (vol. 3, 262) also attributes a criticism of astrology to the Prophet: "Those who say, 'the rain that we receive comes from the kindness of God and from His mercy' believe in me and do not believe in the stars, but those who say 'the rain that we receive comes from a star' do not believe in me but believe in the stars." Quoted by Sayili, *Observatory*, 31.

Figure 4
Circumpolar Star Trails
(Lick Observatory)

It is He Who maketh the stars (as beacons) for you,
That ye may guide yourselves, with their help,
Through the dark spaces of land and sea:
We detail Our Signs for people who know.
– Qur'an (6:97)

CHAPTER 5

MISSING YEARS IN THE HISTORY OF SCIENCE

Everything has got a weapon and the weapon of the believer is his intellect. Everything has got a mainstay and the mainstay of man is his intellect. Everything has got a support and the support of religion is intellect. Every people have got a goal and the goal of this people is intellect. Every people have got a mission and the mission of this people is intellect. – *al-Ghazali* [109]

American history and science texts in the public schools have little to say about science during the period from the seventh through the fifteenth centuries. At best, they call these "Dark Ages" the period in which the "Arabs" preserved ancient Greek thought. In reality, it was the time in which the entire Muslim civilization (Arabs, Africans, Persians, etc.) were absorbing the knowledge of every culture with which they made contact, digesting it, evaluating it, expanding it and breaking out in new directions with it.

The Arabs who brought Islam to the rest of the world were, at the beginning, unschooled in the sciences. They had to make the people to whom they brought Islam their teachers. Thus, at first, the infant Islamic science bore a resemblance to the Greek and other progenitors from which it sprang.

[F]ollowing Aristotle, those who wrote scientific works in Arabic distinguished between the "mathematical" and "physical" sciences. The former group were concerned

---

[109] al-Ghazali, *Ihya*. vol. 1, 112.

with quantity ... whereas the latter dealt with things that possess a principle of motion, such as the elements, whose inherent properties of lightness and heaviness are responsible for their natural motion upward or downward. The distinction was not clear-cut, however. Aristotle himself classified astronomy, optics, and music among "the more physical" of the mathematical sciences, thereby recognizing the existence of sciences of a mixed character.[110]

We have already explained how the Qur'an set the stage for the elevation of the science of the study of the natural world in contrast to the Greek conception of the superiority of mathematics. As Islamic science evolved, the scientists "stressed even more strongly ... the subordination of mathematics to natural science. Mathematics had become a propaedeutical step towards physics, which was no longer considered the lowliest science, tainted by corruptible matter and fleeting appearances."[111]

During the Muslim era, astronomy moved from the realm of the mathematical sciences to that of the physical sciences. The Pythagorean notion "that reality, including music and astronomy, is, at its deepest level, mathematical in nature...." found a ready reception in medieval Christian Europe.[112] The Muslims actively sought physical interpretation of astronomy.

The tendency toward the "physical" interpretation of the heavens was already evident in the writings of the

---

[110] Abdelhamid I. Sabra, "The Exact Sciences," in *The Genius of Arab Civilization: Source of Renaissance*. John Richard Hayes, ed., MIT Press: Cambridge, 1978, 121.

[111] Taton, *History of Science*, 389.

[112] Thus, it is unsurprising that while Ptolemy's *Almagest*, which represents the heavenly spheres as geometrical forms, survived in the original Greek, his more physical representation of astronomy, *Planetary Hypotheses* came intact to Europe only in Arabic and Hebrew translations. Only a part of Book 1 survived in the original Greek. For the Pythagorean notion, see Holger Thessleff, "Pythagorus." In the *Encyclopaedia Britannica, Macropaedia*, v. 15.

third/ninth-century astronomer and mathematician Thābit Ibn Qurrah, especially in his essay on the constitution of the heavens. Although the original of this treatise seems to have been lost, excerpts in the works of many later writers, including Maimonides and Albert Magnus, suggest that Thābit ibn Qurrah had conceived of the heavens as solid spheres with a compressible fluid between the orbs and the eccentrics.[113]

We shall look at this journey in more detail later. First, let us review highlights of some of the scientific breakthroughs made by the Islamic scholars prior to the time of al-Biruni. Some of these breakthroughs laid the groundwork and provided the tools for all that was to follow. Others, in fields unrelated to astronomy, I mention only to illustrate how wide-ranging was original scientific research at the time.

Surely, the most critical development in science in the last two thousand years was the development of "zero" as a placeholder. Without this breakthrough in arithmetic, it is impossible to imagine how a general quantitative science could develop as it has. Not only would calculations be cumbersome and avoided, but devices such as the computer on which I typed this manuscript would have no basis for development. Zero is half of the concept of computer memory and information representation which consists of nothing but ones and zeros!

The use of zero as a placeholder appears to have originated in India. The early Muslim scholars who used it referred to the system as "Indian" numerals, as we today call them "Arabic numerals." The Muslims developed this idea by introducing invaluable extensions and applications to the concept. For example, Abu al-Hasan bin Ibrahim al-Uqlidisi of Damascus (*flourished* about 950)

---

[113] Nasr, *Science and Civilization,* 176.

introduced the idea of decimal fractions, and Jamshid Gayath ad-Din al-Kashi of Persia (*fl.* 1420) applied them generally.[114] He calculated the value of pi to 16 decimal places by an iterative scheme of his own invention. By such techniques, "the mathematicians of the Middle East were able to produce numerical tables of trigonometric and other functions with a reliability and precision unprecedented in their time."[115]

Muhammad ibn Musa al-Khwarizmi (*d. c.* 863) of Baghdad, the author of the first Arabic handbook on what are now called Arabic numerals, provided the world with the tool that made all   the physical sciences subject to quantitative analysis. Our word "algorithm" is an anglicization of al-Khwarizmi's name. The word "algebra" comes from the Arabic word *al-jabr*, which appears in the title of his book on the subject, *Hisāb al-Jabr wa-l-Muqābala*, which can be translated "Calculus of Transposition and Simplification."[116] This book contains "the earliest known treatment of the quadratic equation in one unknown which is at once exhaustive, reasonably rigorous (for its time), and numerical in inception."[117] This work was surpassed by Ibn Badr's *Concise Work on Algebra*, in which he, among other things, "generalizes the rule of the powers ... and introduces irrational numbers."[118] Later Umar Khayyam sought to give cubic equations an exhaustive treatment. Although the subject of algebra existed before the Islamic era, these and other significant steps in solving such "polynomial equations" were contributions of Islamic civilization.

---

[114] Sabra, "The Exact Sciences;" and Edward S. Kennedy, "The Arabic Heritage in the Exact Sciences." *Al Habath* 23 (1970): 327.

[115] See Kennedy, "The Arabic Heritage."

[116] Rashed, "Islamand the Flowering," 135

[117] See Kennedy, "The Arabic Heritage."

[118] Ahmed Djebbar, "A Panorama of Research on the History of Mathematics in al-Andalus and the Maghrib Between the Ninth and Sixteenth Centuries." in *Enterprise of Science in Islam.* Hogendijk and Sabra, eds., 322.

One fascinating mathematical breakthrough was motivated by an interest in the Arabic language. In Arabic, all verbs, nouns, adjectives and adverbs are derived from roots of three or four letters. When these words are written, some of the letters are written out and other signs (such as short vowels) are unwritten. Apparently motivated by the question of how many possible ways there are to read n written letters "taking into account all the unwritten signs of a given language" Ibn Mu'im developed new methods of combinatorial arithmetic. His new results, achieved by new methods, mark "the end of the stage of calculation by means of tables, and the beginning of a new stage, the substitution of arithmetic formulas for these tables."[119] The power of such combinatorial formulas manifested themselves in solving problems in such different fields as "magic squares, inheritance, grammar, and even religion."[120]

As with many other sciences, Islamic medicine started with the absorption of the Greek legacy into Islamic methodology.

> Almost all the healing arts in Islam were indebted more to the indefatigable efforts of Hunayn bin Ishaq al-'Ibadi (809-873) and his team of translators than to any other ninth century author or educator. Together with his students and associates, Hunayn made the most important medical writings of the Greeks available in Arabic ... and established a solid foundation for the development of Arabic medicine by devising a distinctive methodology, which was followed, modified, and perfected during the following century.[121]

---

[119] Djebbar, "Panorama." 325.

[120] Djebbar, "Panorama." 326.

[121] Sami K Hamarneh, "The Life Sciences." in *The Genius of Arab Civilization: Source of Renaissance*. John Richard Hayes, ed., MIT Press: Cambridge, 1978, 145.

Subsequently, Muhammad ibn Zakariya ar-Razi (Latin: Rhazes, 865-925) produced a classic treatise on medical care, a comprehensive medical encyclopedia that "provided considerable insights into the methods, applications, and scope of internal, clinical and psychiatric medicine.... Recognizing the relationship between psyche and soma, he attempted to treat diseases of both mind and body."[122]

More breakthroughs followed: Ibn Butlan's (*d.* 1068) ground-breaking work on preventive health care, Ibn al-Jazzar's (*d. c.* 984) work on prenatal care, and Ibn Zuhr's (*d.* 1162) work on medical experimentation and bedside observation.[123]

Relying on both observations and rational analysis, Abu`Ali al-Husain ibn Sina (Avicenna, 980-1037) was able to determine the existence of the circulation of the blood,[124] later articulated by Ibn an-Nafis (*d.* 1288), and to describe it and relate it to such observable phenomena as the pulse and heartbeat.[125]

Pioneering in the use of local anesthetics and antiseptics, Muslim physicians achieved such skill and advances that they were able to perform cataract surgery on one-eyed patients with

---

[122] See previous note.

[123] See previous note.

[124] Hundreds of years later when William Harvey "discovered" the circulation of the blood, Moliere would satirize the reluctance of contemporary European physicians to accept it in the comedy *Le Malade Imaginaire.* Harvey was an Englishman but studied all the great anatomists, including Ibn Sina, at the University of Padua at the same time Galileo was making a name for himself in that city. At the heavily Islamic-influenced university, he learned something even more important than the fact that blood circulated: he learned induction. Harvey wrote: "I profess both to learn and to teach anatomy, not from books but from dissections; not from the positions of the philosophers but *from* the fabric of nature...." (William Harvey, "An Anatomical Disquisition on the Motion of the Heart and Blood in Animals." in *Great Books*, v. 28. 268.) Thus Harvey was able to build on the work of the past and do for medicine what Galileo was doing for astronomy.

[125] See A. C. Crombie, *Science, Optics, and Music in Medieval and Early Modern Thought.* London: Hambledon, 1990.

confidence. It was in the Islamic civilization that the first hospitals were established and the quarantine introduced to combat the spread of contagious disease.[126]

The contrast between Islamic and medieval European attitudes towards medical science is illustrated in the reports of Usamah Ibn Munqidh, a twelfth-century Muslim world traveler from Syria, that in medieval Europe patients were often treated by priests without any knowledge of medical science. Even European "physicians" seemed more influenced by theologically-tinged superstition than by clinical research. Usamah learned the following story from an Arab Christian physician who had offered to treat a woman afflicted with imbecility. The physician prescribed a change of diet, but a European physician protested his methods. The European diagnosed the problem as a demon in the woman's head and ordered her hair be shaved off. She returned to her normal diet (of garlic and mustard), and her condition worsened.

> The physician then said, "The devil has penetrated her head." He therefore took a razor, made a deep cruciform incision on it, peeled off the skin at the middle of the incision until the bone of the skull was exposed and rubbed it with salt. The woman ... expired instantly.[127]

Despite his low opinion of European medicine in general, it is significant that Usamah did adopt those popular remedies he found there which he judged to be safe and effective.

Note that the Arab physician quoted above was a Christian. I remind the reader that not all the scientists who contributed to

---

[126] Lane, *Islam*, 25-26.

[127] Usamah Ibn Munqidh 12th c., *Memoirs of an Arab Syrian Gentleman or An Arab Knight in the Crusades*. Philip K. Hitti, trans. New York: Columbia Univ. Press, 2000, 162

the Islamic Golden Age were themselves Muslims.[128] Many were Jews and Christians. They benefited from the Islamic culture in which they worked in two respects: (1) they were influenced by the dominant Islamic attitude towards scientific research; and (2) they were free to pursue their work in a way that religious minorities never before in history had been accorded–and rarely have been since, until the American era.

We have mentioned the use of antiseptics in Islam. Hygiene was generally very important in Islam. In medieval Europe, bathing was not a common practice. At the dawn of the modern era, European doctors resisted the suggestion that they should wash between patients. For the Muslim, bathing and washing were articles of faith. Lane remarks that cleanliness was the one issue about which Muhammad could be called a fanatic, insisting that the five-times daily prayers were invalid if the Muslim were not physically clean when he did them. When the Europeans encountered the Islamic world in the Crusades, they found a people who seemed to be constantly bathing even to the extreme of washing their hands between courses of a meal. When the Inquisition took hold of Spain, one of the signs used to spot insincere converts to Christianity was excessive washing.

---

[128] It has been a matter of some controversy how to identify these scholars. Most writers have chosen to identify them as "Arabs" because they all wrote in Arabic, the lingua franca of the Islamic civilization. While this is reasonable, it obscures the often-overlooked fact that they were of many different nationalities, spread out from Spain to China. Rose Wilder Lane (see Lane, *Islam*) chose to call them Saracens to avoid the confusion of calling them all Arabs simply because they wrote in Arabic or Muslims because they happened to live in the Islamic civilization. Some dislike the use of the term Saracen, because of the negative stereotype the word conjures in Western minds. Unfortunately, the words "Arab" and "Muslim" also conjure negative stereotypes in the Western mind. I prefer to use the term "Muslim" because, as I explained earlier, I believe that those scholars benefited from the Islamic culture whether or not they subscribed to the Muslim religion.

The Muslim society practiced scientific farming that produced an abundance of agricultural goods that Europe, where most of the land lay fallow much of the time, could not match. Out of the Muslim world came many new products and technologies and architectural breakthroughs as well:

> Americans owe directly to the Saracens our southwestern and California architecture, our cotton industry, our asphalt paving, and a long list of such things as beds, table and bed linens, small occasional tables, strawberries, ice-cream. Americans speak Arabic when they say mattress, sofa, cotton, talcum, sugar, sherbet, naphtha, gypsum, benzine.[129]

A major development for our subject was the invention of the modern university (see Chapter 3). The first European universities evolved from institutions called studia generale founded in the twelfth century, while the still flourishing al-Azhar University of Cairo has been in existence since 988 A.D. The first great studium, Salerno, evolved out of a ninth-century school of medicine under Constantine the African (born c. 1020 in Carthage, now Tunisia; *d.* 1087 in Italy).[130]

No less important was the Muslims' use of paper. Paper had been invented in China by Ts'ai Lun in or about 105. Hart ranked Ts'ai Lun as the seventh most influential person in history because of the importance of paper – above Gutenberg, the inventor of the printing press.[131] For over 600 years the Chinese kept the technique for the manufacture of paper a secret. Soon after the Muslims had acquired the secret from workmen captured during the conquest of Samarkand in 753, they put the technique to wide-

---

[129] Lane, *Islam*, 44.

[130] Constantine's translation of Islamic medical works and Arabic versions of Greek medical texts also had a major impact on Western thought.

[131] Michael H. Hart, *One Hundred*.

spread use. They realized the value that paper would have in fulfilling their obligation to disseminate knowledge. In the Prophet's time the verses of the Qur'an were written on scraps of bark and the skins of animals. Now copies of the Qur'an and other texts could be spread throughout the world. Paper was put to use in academia almost immediately.[132] Only four decades after they had acquired the knowledge of paper manufacture, "the first paper factory was set up in Baghdad, and by 1000 the entire Islamic world was enjoying bound books, wrapping paper and paper napkins."[133]

Now let us turn to a more detailed summary of Islamic astronomy in the period in question. As with the other sciences, the Muslims began by translating and studying the scientific legacies inherited from Greece, Babylon, India, China, etc. From the Greek, or Hellenistic, side, they took Ptolemy as the astronomer par excellence. It was the Muslims who gave Ptolemy's *magnum opus,* the name by which it is known today: *The Almagest.*[134] Ptolemy, a second-century Egyptian astronomer, had a brilliant mind, and had developed the ancient astronomical worldview in the form of a powerful and sophisticated mathematical model. This model is able to predict, impressively, the gross movements of the planetary bodies in the sky–as long as you don't look too closely.

Ptolemy accepted the principle that the motion of the heavenly bodies had to be accounted for in terms of uniform motion around the centers of circles. To account for the complex motions of the planets we have mentioned above, Ptolemy departed from a simple circle in several respects:

---

[132] Saliba, *History,* 58.

[133] Joel Mokyr, *The Lever of Riches: Technological Creativity and Economic Progress.* New York: Oxford University Press, 1990.

[134] From the Arabic article *al* (meaning "the") prefixed to the Greek word *magest* (meaning "greatest.")

(1) to account for retrograde motions, he has the planets moving in small epicycles, i.e., portable circles which themselves are centered around moving points called deferents which circle the center of their orbit;

(2) he placed the earth at an offset from the center of the deferent circles;

(3) he cheated on the concept of uniform circular motion by requiring that the motion on the planetary circle be uniform, not as seen from the center, but from a point called the "equant," located opposite the offset at which he placed the earth.

From the above you may think that Ptolemy went to a lot of trouble to try to duplicate observations, and thus, you may wonder how his approach falls short of modern scientific induction. There is no reason to believe that Ptolemy made any effort to test his theory with more rigorous observations. He had "saved the appearances" as he understood them. In his view, the mission of the mathematician is to demonstrate that there is no important discrepancy between a theory of circular motions and the observations.

This is reminiscent of Ockham's Razor: "It is vain to do with more what can be done with fewer." Applied to science this means that between two models that explain the same set of observations equally well, we are to prefer the simpler model. The hypotheses of such a preferred model may not actually be correct, of course. One cannot dispute Bishop Butler's famous dictum: "Everything is what it is and not a thing more nor less." Perhaps reality actually resembles the more complex model. Yet, neither can one dispute that, *as a model*, the simplest one that explains observations equally well is preferred. However, Ptolemy did not say that the simplest model must explain things *equally* well. He said it must not differ in any "important" way from the observations. What constitutes an "important" discrepancy? To the modern scientist any discrepancy for which no reasonable explanation can be offered is important.

Ptolemy's criterion seems to reflect the Platonist's milder regard for the general significance of the sensible world:

> There is no doubt that Plato distinguishes two astronomies, the apparent and the real, the apparent being related to the real in exactly the same way as practical (applied) geometry which works with diagrams is related to the real geometry.[135]

As we noted in Chapter 3, Ptolemy does not seem to have looked closely enough at, for example, precession. We mentioned the dispute between Robert Newton and Owen Gingerich as to whether Ptolemy's alleged observations were fraudulent. Although one observation that Ptolemy characterized as carefully made was off by thirty hours, Gingerich objects to calling his report fraudulent.[136] If it is not fraud, it certainly indicates that Ptolemy's conception of a "careful" observation (or of an "important" difference between theory and observation) was different from that of modern scientists. It was also different from that which emerged among astronomers of the classical Islamic era.

Muslim astronomers aimed at increasing precision of observational measurements both by increasing the size of the measuring instruments and by inventing new devices (e.g., Ibn Sina "invented a device which is in principle equivalent to a micrometer") and methods[137] (e.g. al-Biruni developed a forerunner to the "method of transversals" that modern Westerners associate with Tycho Brahe).[138] Even Ibn Yunus, who preferred portable instruments, in

---

[135] Sir Thomas Heath, *Aristarchus of Samos: a History of Greek Astronomy to Aristarchus.* Oxford: Oxford University Press, 1913, 138.

[136] Robert R. Newton, *Ancient Astronomical Observations;* Owen Gingerich, "Ptolemy Revisited."

[137] Sayili, *Observatory*, 125, citing E. Weidemann, *liber ein von Ibn Sina Hergestelltes Beobachtungsinstrument, Zeitschrift für Instrumentkunde,* 1925, 270-271ff.

[138] Sayili, *Observatory*, 125, citing Fritz Schmidt. *Geschichte der Geodätischen Instrumenten und Verfahren in Altertum und Mittelalter,* 1935, 26, 266, 280.

part preferred them because of the imprecision introduced into large instruments by deformations.[139]

As we have said, the study of the signs in the heavens was a repeated commandment in the Qur'an. Islamic astronomers worked "in their own houses or on nearby hills or even used minarets as in the case of the Giralda tower in Seville, which is said to have been used for this purpose by Jābir ibn Afla<u>h</u>."[140] From a simple beginning generating almanacs in the seventh century, Islamic civilization went on to develop observational enterprises of an impressive scale:[141]

> Observational activity, which began as early as the eighth century, was quite impressive, though largely divorced from theoretical developments. It was given strong impetus at the time of Caliph Abdullah al-Ma'mun (813-833) who ordered the preparation of new astronomical tables (or *zijes*). The result was the influential *Ma'munic zij*, which was based on observational and computational instruments, such as astrolabes, quadrants, and armillaries of various centers of astronomical research in the Islamic world–at Shiraz (by`Abd ar-Rahman as-Sufi, *d.* 986), Cairo (by Ibn Yunus, died 1009), Ghazna (by al-Biruni, died after 1050), Maragha (by al-Tusi and his collaborators), and Samarkand (by Ulugh Beg, *d.* 1449), to mention only a few of those centers.... Considerable effort went into designing and constructing of ever more precise and more sophisticated observational and computational instruments ... of various

---

[139] Sayili, *Observatory*, 126.

[140] Nasr, *Science and Civilization,* 112.

[141] The word "almanac" comes from the Arabic *al-man'kh* which means climate. These 7th century tables predicted probable weather conditions from the climatic impact of the earth's position in its orbit, much as their descendent The Old Farmers' Almanac does today.

types. The description of an instrument constructed in the thirteenth century at Maragha by the Damascene astronomer al-'Urdi has been compared to a similar one made and used in the sixteenth century by Tycho Brahe.[142]

The work of Ibn Yunus is of particular interest since the surviving manuscripts of his *Hakīmī Zīj* are prefaced with many actual observations. In most cases, the observations upon which a *zīj* is based, even if identified (see, e.g., Debarnot 1987), are not preserved.

One fascinating thing about the Muslim astronomical research was the degree to which repeated observations were made.[143] It is remarkable because they did not have the modern understanding of statistics that allows for a precise quantification for how the error in the estimation of a mean value goes down with an increasing number of observations (see footnote 86). Despite the fact that they did not have a quantified theory of error they were well aware that an increased number of observations qualitatively reduces the uncertainty.[144] And their individual observations attained a precision "close to the limit of resolution of the unaided eye."[145] Whether accumulating observations or simply striving for accuracy with each observation, the Muslim astronomers were in accord with

---

[142] Sabra, "The Exact Sciences."

[143] E.g., Sayili, *Observatory*, 96, 138-39, 177.

[144] I was not aware of this when I wrote the first edition of my book. Since then I have found this quote from Gayath ad-Din: "The ascertainment with accuracy of the mean positions and the equations, and likewise, of the configurations in latitude and other matters concerning stellar bodies is humanly impossible; it is permissible, nevertheless, to try to attain to the maximum of precision so as not to allow any approximations in calculations to cause additional divergences exceeding observable quantities." Sayili, *Observatory*, 81.

[145] F. R. Stephenson and L. V. Morrison, "Precision of Islamic Eclipse Measurements." *Journal History of Astronomy.* 22 (1991): 195.

the Qur'anic injunctions cited in Chapter 3. Such precision was not exceeded in Europe until the sixteenth century with the work of Tycho Brahe.[146]

In addition to repeated observations, the Muslims engaged in simultaneous observations at widely spaced locations. These were especially valuable in determining the elusive parameter of earthly longitudes. Al Biruni and Abul Wafa Muhammad ibn Ahmad al Buzjani made coordinated observations of the lunar eclipse of 387 (997 C.E.), and found an approximately one hour time difference between Baghdad and al-Khwarazm.[147]

The fruits of these observations could be seen in the high precision of the improved measurements of the planetary orbital parameters. For example, al-Biruni's listing of the period of Saturn in his *Ghurrat-uz-Zijāt* differs by less than 7 parts in one hundred thousand from the modern value.[148]

As the precision of these measurements of planetary positions and motions improved, astronomers were confronted with the challenge to refine Ptolemy's model into better agreement with

[146] Kremer (see R. L. Kremer, "Bernard Walthen's Astronomical Observations," Journal History of Astronomy 11 (1980): 174) notes, "No one has yet attempted to study, systematically, medieval astronomical observations, Latin or Arabic." He estimates a positional accuracy for the work of the fifteenth century observer Bernard Walthen of about 6 minutes of arc. Stephenson and Morrison, "Precision," cite a value of 2.8 minutes of arc for al-Biruni and 0.6 minutes of arc for Bani Musa. Sayili, *Observatory* reports that Abd al Rahman al Sufi used an observing ring with marks at 5 arc minutes.

[147] Sayili, *Observatory*, 10.

[148] Saiyid Samad Husein Risvi, "Portraits of Two Savants and Humanists–Bīrūnī and Albert the Great." in Al-Biruni *Commemorative Volume: Proceedings of the International Congress Held in Pakistan.* ed. H. M. Said. Karachi: Hamdard, 1979, 195.

their measurements, or to overthrow it for another.[149] Let us review some of the general advances made by the Muslims in astronomy and then look closely at the problem of how planets move and the impact this question has had for modern science.

The development of mathematics at the beginning of the Islamic era was closely tied to astronomy. The Muslims learned of the sine function from Indian astronomy. Out of this function they developed, in the ninth century, all the other standard trigonometric functions. The further development of trigonometry, at first, took place within the sphere of astronomy and the work is found in astronomical treatises. It was the great astronomer, Nasir ad-Din at-Tusi, who made spherical trigonometry into a separate branch of mathematics.[150] At-Tusi was the director of the great observatory at Maragha (Persia) commissioned by Ghengis Khan's grandson Hulagu. Although Hulagu appears to have been motivated by his belief in astrology,[151] in at-Tusi's hands, the observatory marked a new phase in the development of astronomical research. It was a full-fledged scientific research institution in the modern sense, with an endowment,[152] a library of "400,000 volumes"[153] reputedly

---

[149] The question as to whether the differences between the observational predictions of the Islamic models and those of Ptolemy were discernible is not settled. At-Tusi noted that his system differed from Ptolemy's in that it produced a "bulge" across the orbit of a planet between its farthest and closest approaches. (Copernicus' model also differs from Ptolemy's in this way since it is at-Tusi's model with the sun moved to the center.) At-Tusi quantified this bulge and declared that the difference is an "imperceptible amount" (ghayr mahsūs). Ragep (see F. Jamil Ragep, "The Two Versions of the Tūsī Couple." in *From Deferent to Equant: A Volume of Studies in the History of Science in the Ancient and Medieval Near East in Honor of E. S. Kennedy*. David A. King and George Saliba, eds. New York: New York Academy of Sciences, 1987) notes that although this difference is unquestionably imperceptible in most cases, the assertion that it is imperceptible in the case of Mars–where it is quite large–"would certainly be an interesting topic to pursue." The unusually high eccentricity (departure from circularity) of Mars' orbit provided Kepler with the data he needed to establish the fact that planetary orbits are elliptical, once he had Tycho Brahe's precise observational data.

[150] Sabra, "The Exact Sciences."

[151] Sayili, *Observatory*, 202-3.

[152] Sayili, *Observatory*, 207.

[153] Sayili, *Observatory*, 194.

"collected from Baghdad, Syria and Al Jazira,"[154] "well equipped with astronomical instruments,"[155] and a renowned international staff.[156] For example, it included a mural quadrant (a device for measuring the position of astronomical bodies) marked in minutes of arc and an instrument for measuring the apparent diameter of the moon and sun.[157] Perhaps five years in the making,[158] the Maragha institution was more than a mere observatory, it "was a complex scientific institution, in which nearly every branch of science was taught, and where some of the most famous scientists of the medieval period were assembled."[159]

Another interesting aspect of at-Tusi's work is that he was aware of the observational errors in his work. By that I don't mean that he committed blunders, but rather that his work had an uncertainty due to the limits of precision in any scientific study. For example, there is an inherent error in the limited precision of the instruments one uses. Thus, he states that a certain difference between his theory and Ptolemy's of 1/6th of a degree is "imperceptible."[160]

---

[154] Sayili, *Observatory*, 205.

[155] Nasr, *Science and Civilization*, 81.

[156] Sayili, *Observatory*, 205-207.

[157] Sayili, *Observatory*, 199.

[158] Sayili, *Observatory*, 196.

[159] Nasr, *Science and Civilization*, 81.

[160] See F. Jamil Ragep, "The Two Versions of the Tūsī Couple." The theory of error is an important part of modern science. Islamic astronomers were aware of the importance of knowing what the uncertainties in their research was. Modern error theory is based on a sophisticated understanding of statistics that the medieval Muslims lacked. This statistical knowledge was largely developed by modern mathematicians' analyses of games of chance. Could Islam's disapproval of games of chance have been an inhibiting factor in the development of statistics by Islamic mathematicians?

At-Tusi was not unique among the Muslim astronomers in this respect.[161] There was a heightened awareness of the significance of including consideration of observational uncertainty that distinguished Islamic astronomy from the work of Greek scientists even of the revered stature of Galen. Consider al-Ghazali's attack on Galen's "proof" that the Sun was eternal:

> Said [Galen]: If the Sun were liable to annihilation, signs of decay in it would be visible in course of time. But the astronomical observation of its size has for thousands of years revealed the same quantity. If, therefore, it has not decayed through these long ages, it follows that it is incorruptible.
>
> ... [E]ven if it is granted that there is no corruption without decay, how did Galen know that the decay has not befallen the Sun? His reference to astronomical observations is absurd. For quantities discovered by astronomical observation are only approximate. If the Sun, which is said to be one hundred and seventy times as big as the Earth, or any other thing of the same size as the Sun loses as much as a range of hills, the loss cannot be apparent to the senses. So it may be assumed that the Sun is in decay and that so far it has lost as much as a range of hills, or a little more; and that the human sense cannot perceive this loss, for in the human sciences which depend on observation quantities are known only approximately.[162]

---

[161] Al-Biruni showed awareness of error inherent in instrumentation when he preferred certain earlier latitude measurements to his own on the grounds that his instrumental errors are larger. See Nafis Ahmad, "Some Glimpses of Al-Bīrūnī." in Al-Bīrūnī[w] *Commemorative Volume: Proceedings of the International Congress Held in Pakistan,* ed. H. M. Said, Karachi: Hamdard, 1979, 141.

[162] al-Ghazali c. 1095, in *Al-Ghazali's Tahāfut Al-Falāsifah [Incoherence of the Philosophers].* Sabih Ahmad Kamali, trans., Lahore: Sheikh, 1963.

While Tusi was correct in stating that the theoretical difference between his predictions and those of Ptolemy's were imperceptible, he was mistaken to assume that Ptolemy's theoretical positions matched the observations. For example, we have no evidence that Ptolemy measured the planetary positions other than at the their conjunction (point closest to the sun), opposition (point farthest from the sun), epicyclic perigee (point on the epicycle nearest the earth) and epicyclic apogee (point on the epicycle farthest from the earth). As Muslim astronomers became increasingly critical of Ptolemy, Mu'ayyad al-Din al-'Urdi (*d.* 1266) would propose a model in which the trajectory of the moon's motion differed from Ptolemy's at the intervening points.[163]

The Muslims also made advances in the measuring and mapping of the world. The Greek Eratosthenes devised a method for determining the size of the earth by measuring the distance between two places on the earth's surface and the length of the arc between them on the assumption that the earth has a spherical surface. Ignoring the fact that the earth is not a perfect sphere, the ratio of the distances between the two locations to the circumference of the earth is the same as the difference in latitudes to 360 degrees. An expedition commissioned by Caliph Ma'mun, applied Eratosthenes' technique with such precision that they obtained a result within 1% of the modern value.

Later, al-Biruni (*d.* 1050), noted for his work on measuring the latitudes and longitudes of geographical locations, devised an ingenious method for determining the size of the earth.[164] Avoiding the expeditions involved in Eratosthenes' technique, he simply climbed a mountain whose height he had determined by simple trigonometry and measured the angle dip of the horizon. The measurement was made with an instrument of his own devising. He compared the

---

[163] Dallal, Astronomical Work of Sadr, 314.
[164] Nafis Ahmad, "Some Glimpses of Al-Bīrūnī," 141.

measurement against a model for the size of the earth using sine tables that he himself had calculated. He appears to have made a correction for the effects of refraction by the air. At the end, the value he calculated for the earth's curvature at the place where the measurements were made differ by less than one-fifth of a percent from the modern value. This fine agreement is partly fortuitous. From the instrumental errors alone we would expect a precision of only about 1%. The point here is that the observations were made with extreme care. In contrast, it was not until Isaac Newton's day that Europeans accepted a value even close to that calculated by al-Biruni.[165] Al-Biruni documented this measurement in his *Kitāb Taḥdīd al-Amākin* as a prefatory step in the determination of the longitude difference between Mecca and Ghazna. Accurate longitude determinations were an extremely difficult task in the era before the development of modern timepieces.[166] Historian of science E. S. Kennedy, author of a detailed commentary on the *Taḥdīd*,[167] calls al-Biruni's achievement in the case of Mecca to Ghazna "a masterpiece of applied science."[168]

The importance that scientific precision has in the rise and fall of theories cannot be overstated. In the ninth century, al-Battani's measurements of the motions of the heavenly bodies made it possible for later astronomers to measure the gradual changes in the moon's motion over the centuries. He, himself, determined that the "line of Apsides" (the line through the earth and sun when they are furthest apart in their orbit) changes with time. He also corrected Ptolemy's error in the rate of precession. Al-Battani used trigonometric rather

---

[165] Saiyid Samad Husein Risvi, "Portraits of Two Savants and Humanists–Bīrūnī and Albert the Great."

[166] See Jamil Ali, *The Determination of the Coordinates of Cities, Al-Bīrūnī's Tahdid al-Am'kin.* Beirut: Centenniel Publ. Univ. of Beirut, 1967.

[167] E. S. Kennedy, *A Commentary upon Bīrūnī's Kitāb Tahdīd al-Amākin.* Beirut: American Univ. of Beirut, 1973.

[168] E. S. Kennedy, private communication (1992).

than the geometrical methods of Ptolemy. He was able to show that variations of the distance between the earth and the sun would require the possibility of annular eclipses as well as solar eclipses. He and his many successors would severely challenge the whole Ptolemaic theory.[169]

We have seen how the tools of astronomical research developed in the Islamic world. We shall next look at one particular problem that is most associated with the rise of modern science. The question of how planets move might seem as far removed from earthly concerns as one can get. Yet, the scientific revolution in which this question eventually culminated has become the prototype for understanding scientific revolutions, and other revolutions as well. It led to the popularity of the concept of the "paradigm."

Thomas Kuhn used the word "paradigm" to refer to a general perspective, a body of theories by which we view the world.[170] What Westerners know as the "Copernican" paradigm, as opposed to the "Ptolemaic" paradigm, is an almost literal example of this concept. If you start by looking at the earth as fixed and immovable body at the center of the universe, your entire worldview is different from looking at the earth as just another of innumerable bodies whirling around in a vast space. It is not a matter of replacing a single theory with another, but of changing one's total frame of reference.

---

[169] "While al-Battani takes no critical attitude towards the Ptolemaic kinematics in general, he evidences ... a very sound scepticism in regard to Ptolemy's practical results. Thus, relying on his own observations, he corrects–be it tacitly, be it in open words—Ptolemy's errors. This concerns the main parameters of planetary motion no less than erroneous conclusions drawn from insufficient or faulty observations, such as the invariability of the obliquity of the ecliptic or of the solar apogee." Hartner's article on al-Battani in *Dictionary of Scientific Biography*. New York 1970-1990 as quoted by J. J. O'Connor and E. F. Robertson, "Abu Abdallah Mohammad ibn Jabir Al-Battani." *Biographies*. St. Andrews, Scotland: Univ. of St. Andrews, 2003, http://www-gap.dcs.st-and.ac.uk/history/Mathematicians/Al-Battani.html (accessed 8/29/03).

[170] Thomas Kuhn, *The Structure of Scientific Revolutions*. Chicago: Univ. of Chicago, 1970.

We too often think of the change from the geocentric (earth-centered) to the heliocentric (sun-centered) universe as a single event in time. It was the climax of a process of investigation and criticism that took many centuries. The paradigm shift from earth-centered to sun-centered cosmology was a step in a much more comprehensive paradigm shift from a dualistic physical reality to a physical reality of a single set of universal laws. The truly revolutionary question is not which body sits at the center of the universe, but whether the universe has a center at all. Scholars had disputed over what was at the center of the universe before. The idea that the sun was at the center of the universe had been considered by the ancient Greeks, and had been accepted by Aristarchus. Pythagoras believed that there was a great fire at the center of the universe about which both the sun and earth orbited. Although it did not run its course until the seventeenth century, the idea that there is no "natural place" for things in the universe emerged during the Islamic era. It climaxed with Isaac Newton's demonstration of the principle that all physical laws are universal. That principle had been proposed centuries earlier by al-Biruni in a debate with ibn Sina over whether heavenly bodies were subject to the same law of gravity as terrestrial objects (see p. 102). With the universal theory of gravity and the laws of motion, Newton established the new paradigm. In the twentieth century, it has been taken a step further with Einstein's theory that not only is there no natural *place* in the universe–there is no natural "reference frame" either.

Although astronomy and physics have changed in revolutionary ways since Al-Biruni and even Newton, the idea that physical laws are the same throughout space is still part of the prevailing paradigm. In astronomy it appears in the form of a working hypothesis called the "cosmological principle" that viewed on a sufficiently large scale there are no preferred places or directions in the universe. Einstein's theory of relativity, though revolutionary, only alters our understanding of *which* physical quantities are invariant. Contrary to the glib phrase sometimes thrown out by nonscientists attempting to (mis)apply the theory of relativity to philosophy, Einstein did not prove that "everything is relative." He demonstrated the consequences of the assumption that the speed of light is an *absolute constant*, in other words, that it is not relative.[171] The physical implications of this assumption for the nature space and time appear to be confirmed by the observations.

When we look at the sky, we have the distinct feeling that the sky is turning around us. The sun rises in the east and sets in the west, as do the stars and planets on a daily basis. At night we see Polaris, the pole star, stay in the same place all night as the other stars seem to crawl in a circular parade around it. (See Figure 4.) We can easily imagine that the sky is a great dome turning around the earth, located at its center. Of course, it could be that the earth itself is a round ball turning around its own axis so that all those other objects just *seem* to be rotating around us on a daily basis. Which is the case?

The school of Pythagoras set the tone for the deductive approach to astronomy. To the Pythagoreans, the harmony of numbers held the key to the harmony of the heavenly spheres. Their name for the heavens was the *kosmos* (from which our modern word cosmos is derived), which is Greek for "harmony." For them, the sublime outermost sphere containing the "fixed stars" rotated in a perfect daily circular motion.

The stars form patterns called constellations, which make it easy for one to learn one star from another. For example, everyone has heard of the "Big Dipper" and can learn to spot it in the sky. Watching the handle of the Big Dipper turn like a clock's hour hand at night you would find it easy to believe that the Pythagoreans are right.

---

[171] Albert Einstein, *Relativity: The Special and the General Theory: A Popular Exposition.* New York: Crown, 1961.

Yet some of the bright objects in the sky do not move in perfect time with the fixed stars. Watching the sky from one night to the next, one could see the "planets" (from the Greek word meaning "wanderer") wandering away from this perfect daily motion. For example, the moon drifts from one constellation to another in a belt of twelve constellations called the zodiac until, after a month, it is back where it started, changing its phase as it does so:

And the Moon,–
We have measured for her
Mansions (to traverse)
Till she returns
Like the old (and withered)
Lower part of a date-stalk.
    – Qur'an (36:39)

When the moon is very near the sun, it is lost from sight in the glare of the sun. It first becomes visible as a very thin crescent. As it moves around the earth the angle between it and the sun changes so that we see more and more of its full face. It waxes into the first quarter, gibbous, and full phase, as indicated in Figure 6. As it swings back towards the sun, it wanes, going through the last quarter phase and then to the famished and wasted old crescent so nicely described in the Qur'anic passage above.

The Sun, too, drifts, more slowly, taking a year to get back where it started. The Pythagoreans could crudely account for such motions by placing within the sphere of fixed stars lesser shells for each of the planets with their own circular motion relative to the outermost starry sphere. As appealing as this model may have been to the Pythagoreans' love of circular motion, it just doesn't match the motion of the planets, even as they were known to the ancient Greeks.

The other planets, Mercury, Venus, Mars, Jupiter and Saturn, did not simply drift in one direction against the background stars. Every once in a while, a planet would turn around and drift the other way! This is called "retrograde motion" by the astronomers. After a while, the planet will stop and again return to its original direction.

Plato, as we have noted, viewed the material world as an imperfect reflection of perfect forms. He held that the purpose of astronomy is to "save the appearances" of the real world planets' bizarre motions by accounting for them in terms of perfectly uniform circular motions. His friend and student, Eudoxus, took up the challenge and made a complicated model of 27 moving spheres centered on the earth, with three or four spheres dedicated to explaining the motions of each of the planets (spheres within spheres, like layers of an onion). His model did not fit the actual retrograde motions well,[172] but he influenced that most influential of Greek philosophers, Aristotle.

Aristotle added another 28 spheres to Eudoxus' scheme, but it did not explain the planetary motions any better. In accord with the deductive paradigm, he was motivated by philosophical rather than observational considerations. The additional complication followed from his first principles. Aristotle believed that there are four terrestrial elements and the natural motion of each was towards its respective natural place in the universe: earth to the center, water above that, air above that, and fire rising up above the other three. The heavenly bodies were subject to an entirely different physics. For them, made of the fifth element, the "quintessence," motion naturally tended to circularity. These motions were natural, that is, they required no forces to explain them.[173]

---

[172] The model failed to match other observational data as well; for example, the variations in the brightness of the planets as they move closer or further from the earth.

[173] See Michael Zeilik, Astronomy: *The Evolving Universe*. 9th ed. Cambridge: Cambridge Univ. Press, 2002, 26-27.

The similarity between Aristotle's approach and modern science lies in his concern for the "physics." This is in opposition to Ptolemy's limited concern for modeling the observations ("saving the phenomena") or the physical reality of the components of his theoretical model. We must note, however, that Aristotle's approach departs radically from modern "scientific" method in two important ways: (1) it relies more heavily upon deduction than experiment, and (2) it violates the principle that laws are universal.

Although most of Islamic physics followed Aristotle's lead, there was a group of Muslim scientists whose revolutionary approach marked the transition to modern science in the sense we have described: a greater emphasis on experiment and the concept that physical laws are universal. Although these scientists were few, their work is important in understanding the origins of modern science. They followed the Qur'anic injunctions on methodology and a *tawhīd* (unitarian) cosmological principle rather than imitating Aristotelian style or committing themselves to the dualistic idea that the universe has two regimes where two different sets of law operate. This group included Qutb ad-Din ash-Shirazi, Abu Ali al-Hasan Ibn al-Haytham (Alhazen, 965-1039), al-Biruni, and the freed Greek slave Abu'l-Fath Abd al-Rahman al-Khazini (*fl.* in Merv at the beginning of the 12th century). They are famous for their work in physics, including research on optics, the specific weights of minerals, and gravity.

Seyyed Nasr claims that this group was not the mainstream of Muslim science.[174] I concede that they were exceptional, but they were exceptional in the sense that Newton and Einstein were exceptional in modern times. It is their work that set the trends for modern science. What is important from the viewpoint of understanding Islam and science is that their novel techniques were well-founded in Qur'anic principles. Further, at least in the case of al-Biruni, the intensity of

---

[174] Nasr, *Science and Civilization*, 127.

their religious devotion and their own understanding of its relationship to the quality of their scientific commitment exceeded that of
those scholars who would later be remembered best as commentators
on Aristotle.

> [I]t is not just a question of a savant who happens to be a
> believer ... [al-Biruni's] spirit of scientific research springs
> from, and is rooted in, his faith in God.[175]

Tawhīd, belief in the oneness of God, is the fundamental principle of Islam. It has its corollary in physical science, the belief that
the laws of nature, properly understood, reveal the hand of a single
Creator. Thus, al-Biruni's concept that the laws of physics are the
same throughout all space.

The concern of scientists of the Islamic civilization with the
role of physics in the heavenly regions did not originate with al-
Biruni. Before him, Thabit Ibn Qurrah (826 or 836-901), a Sabaean
translator of Greek works into Arabic, interpreted the Aristotelian
spheres as actual physical entities. Ibn al-Haytham was a pioneer in
experimental method, best known for his revolutionary work on
optics. He developed an experimentally based and mathematically
detailed theory of visual perception.

The Muslims initially had adopted a Greek model of sight, based
on the ideas of Euclid, Galen, and Ptolemy. This model, known as
the "extramission hypothesis," proposed that a sensitive "pneuma"
was emitted by the eye and produced vision by "contact," "coales-
cence," or "cooperation" with external light.[176] In his early career Ibn
Haytham worked within that old model, although his refinements
were impressive. He attempted a reconstruction of a lost book of

---

[175] Gardet, Louis, "Portraits of Two Savants and Humanists—Bīrūnī and Albert the Great."
in *Al-Biruni Commemorative Volume: Proceedings of the International Congress Held in
Pakistan.* H. M. Said, ed., Karachi: Hamdard, 1979, 195.

[176] A. I. Sabra, "Ibn Al-Haytham's Revolutionary Project in Optics: The Achievement and
the Obstacle." In *Enterprise of Science in Islam.* Hogendijk and Sabra, eds., 87.

Ptolemy's that may have inspired a "foundation for Ptolemy's experimental and psychological treatment of a subject which Euclid had dealt with in predominantly geometrical terms."[177] In maturity he produced the Book of Optics (*Kitāb al-Munāzirāt*) that announced "a decisive break with the basic assumptions of earlier mathematicians, including Euclid and Ptolemy."[178] Having been influenced by Ptolemy's work on optics he then became the mathematician to write "the first treatise that superseded it."[179]

Ibn Haytham introduced a coherent and revolutionary new theory in which light is "an independent physical property" that followed experimentally verifiable rules and whose characteristic physical effect on psychological systems of vision initiated specified processes ultimately ending in the visual perception of external objects and of all their visible qualities or properties ... through mental operations of 'inference' (*qiyās, istidlāl*) or interpretation."[180] He felt that felt that his predecessors had confused a rigorous mathematical approach to optics with the "not-so-thorough" approach of natural philosophers. He called for a new synthesis (*tarkīb*).[181] Rather than simply accept existing doctrines, the new synthesis would require "subjecting the relevant 'particulars' and 'properties' (a vision of light) to inspection and then and only then, in the 'gathering by induction (*istiqrā'*) what is found in the manner of vision to be uniform, unchanging and not subject to doubt' (Optics, I, 1[6])."[182]

Ibn al-Haytham's methodology, outlined in his Preface, is quite modern. He begins by describing the "conditions" under which vision takes place, "as revealed by a series of detailed observations supported by carefully described experiments: the existence of distance

---

[177] Sabra, "Ibn Al-Haytham," 90.

[178] See previous note.

[179] See previous note.

[180] Sabra, "Ibn Al-Haytham," 91.

[181] See previous note.

[182] Sabra, "Ibn Al-Haytham," 92, quoting Ibn al-Haytham, *The Optics of Ibn Al-Haytham. I: On Direct Vision.* A.I. Sabra, trans. London: Warbug Institute, 1989.

between eye and object; the existence of unobstructed straight lines between points on the surface of the eye and points on the objects perceived surface; luminosity of the object; a minimum size of the object that varies with the strength of the viewers eyesight; opacity and color of the seen object; and ascertainable variability of distance with the size of the object, the degree of the object's luminosity and color, and with the strength of eyesight."[183] Unlike the theories of his predecessors there are no hidden entities or properties, and the experiments upon which his theory is based are fully preserved in the Arabic texts.[184]

There is, unfortunately, one thing that Ibn Haytham does not subject to rigorous empirical test: the observational claims of his Greek predecessors. He makes the mistake of taking on trust their claims that the crystalline "humor" of the eye–and it alone–is "the 'first' or 'principal' seat of visual 'sensation.'" His own experiments prove that the color and intensity in any point of the crystalline part of the eye consists of a mix of light coming from varying directions. How then can the crystalline sense anything amid visual noise? Rather than doubt the ancients' claim and propose experiments to test it, Ibn Haytham advances the hypothesis that only those rays passing perpendicularly through the crystalline are sensed.[185]

This lapse is not because Ibn Haytham is unaware of the difference between a mathematical and a physical approach to optics. On the contrary, he argues against the "mathematicians" (and Galen) as against the "proponents of physical science." He accounts for the impression that one sees an object outside the eye when the object is actually within the eye by appealing to psychological factors. "[W]ithout discernment and prior knowledge sight would achieve

---

[183] Sabra, "Ibn Al-Haytham," 92.

[184] Sabra, "Ibn Al-Haytham," 97.

[185] Sabra, "Ibn Al-Haytham," 98. The obstacle to understanding vision posed by the belief in crystalline sensitivity was finally removed by Kepler. Sabra, "Ibn Al-Haytham," 110.

no vision whenever." He discusses psychological issues at length, including the illusion that the moon is bigger on the horizon than when it is higher in the sky.[186]

Ibn Haytham believed that before studying a problem one must first consider the opinions of the Ancients, but then one must reject them when they contradict one's own research.[187] His willingness to supercede those claims of the ancients which were based on rational demonstration alone, while being overly credulous of their empirical claims, tells us something about Ibn Haytham's theory of knowledge. Clearly he did not accept the view that unaided reason is a sure guide to knowledge, yet he doesn't seem to appreciate that degree to which the Greeks didn't share his view. Thus, he was skeptical of their work only when they failed to profess to have made observations backing them. Thus, he realizes that Galen's "explanation" of depth perception merely amounts to an assertion that the observed body is simply seen in the place that it is. In contrast, Ibn Haytham gives an inductive analysis of depth perception weighing empirical data against an integrated theory within the framework of his "newly argued concept of an optical image on the common nerve."[188] He concludes that distance is ascertained by "signs" or "cues."[189] His concept of the image in the eye is neither Aristotelian nor Ptolemaic.

David Lindberg remarks that "[m]odern optical thought issues, by direct descent, from the work of Alhazen and his immediate

---

[186] Sabra, "Ibn Al-Haytham,"104. This question is still unsolved.

[187] Gerhard Endress, "Mathematics and Philosophy in Medieval Islam," in Hogendijk and Sabra, *Enterprise of Science in Islam*, 143.

[188] Sabra, "Ibn Al-Haytham," 106.

[189] Sabra, "IbnAl-Haytham," 107.

followers."[190] Among those followers was Kamal ad-Din al-Farsi (*fl.* near end of 13th century) who explained the rainbow for the first time in history, after *experimentally* studying its formation with the use of a simulated raindrop made of a water-filed glass sphere.[191] In his *Resumé of Astronomy*, Ibn al-Haytham criticized those who interpreted the heavens as abstract geometrical forms. He argued that it was possible to transfer the Ptolemaic motions "to plane or spherical surfaces" and produce a "more exact," "more comprehensible," representation and with "shorter" demonstrations.[192]

Ibn al-Haytham is a seminal figure in the development of the process I have been calling "induction." The general principles Ibn al-Haytham seeks are not metaphysical doctrines but "are specific theorems, developed from physical theory, but closer to the facts under discussion."[193] Ibn Haytham calls his method "induction" (*istiqrā*). He does not mean by this merely advancing from particular cases to universal cases (as Aristotle does in *Posterior Analytics*), but "to check the limits of the theoretical model by means of systematic observation (*i'tibār*, experience)."[192] He transforms induction until it becomes

> focused on the refinement of complex procedures, asked to provide criteria for the validity of the models.... The true progress, owing to a true revolution in method, was based on a new conception of the use of mathematics for the dispersion of those particulars, collected and surveyed in order to support a perfect inductive inquiry yielding valid results. While mathematical models are based on the data of observation,

[190] David C. Lindberg, *Studies in the History of Medieval Optics*. London: Variorum Reprints, 1983.

[191] A. C. Crombie, Science, *Optics, and Music*; Sabra, "The Exact Sciences."

[192] Nasr, *Science and Civilization*, 177.

[193] Endress, "Mathematics and Philosophy," 144.

[194] See previous note.

the philosopher-mathematician is convinced of the essential coherence between valid models and the plan—the *logos*— of nature.[195]

Ibn Haytham also criticized Ptolemy's theory of planetary motion. The fact that it did not accord with the motions of the interior planets constituted a violation of "sound principles."[196] He notes that Ptolemy himself seemed to be aware of some of these inconsistencies, but defended them on the grounds that he was "compelled by the nature of our subject to use a procedure not in strict accordance with theory."[197] However, Ibn Haytham didn't see how one could employ the experimental methods that had been so successful in optics in the field of astronomy.[198]

There is a common misconception among Western historians of science that the Muslim objections to the Ptolemaic theory of planetary motion were purely philosophical. To the contrary, George Saliba's study of planetary theories in the calassical Islamic era determined that only al-Bitruji sought to reform Ptolemaic astronomy on philosophical grounds (ending up with a weaker match to the observations).[199] Muslim objections were physical and/or observational.

Aristotle had argued that heavenly things tend to move circularly while earthly things tended to move towards a hypothetical center of the universe. Al-Biruni challenged this analysis and suggested one that required a single set of universal laws and appealed to observation for support. In a letter to the Aristotelian Ibn Sina, al-Biruni argued that the heavens may actually be subjected to a universal law of gravity. He argued that some physical constraint may prevent them from falling towards the earth despite the gravitational pull.

---

[195] See previous note.
[196] Endress, "Mathematics and Philosophy," 147.
[197] See previous note.
[198] Endress, "Mathematics and Philosophy," 148.
[199] George Saliba, *History*, 25.

Aristotle had held that the heavens' "natural place" differed from that of the earth's, with water occupying a middle level. Al-Biruni noted that this was empirically unsound since it is clearly observable that water obeys gravitational laws:

> Furthermore if we allow water to flow freely, taking away any obstacles in its path, undoubtedly it will reach the center; therefore the assertion that the natural place of water is above the earth is without any basis. Consequently, there is no "natural place" for any body. On such a basis, he who says that the heavens are indeed heavy, but that it is their being attached that prevents their falling does not appear absurd.[200]

Al-Biruni conceded that he did not know what the physical mechanism for supporting the heavens was. Much later, Isaac Newton would show that it is *momentum*, a concept developed by Muslim scholars (ironically, including Ibn Sina; see discussion later in this chapter), that counteracts the effect of gravity, which he also conceived to be a *universal* force directly proportional to the product of the masses and inversely proportional to the square of the distances between any two objects in the universe. The inertia of the heavenly bodies, deflected by the gravitational attraction of the sun, results in their elliptical, not circular, motion. While our understanding of gravity has changed since Newton's day, replaced by the newer and more general theory developed by Einstein, al-Biruni's general principle remains the working hypothesis underlying modern science. One set of laws governs all of space-time. Given that there is only one God, it could not have been any other way.

Nasr also gives an example of a letter of al-Biruni to Ibn Sina refuting Aristotle's claim that elliptical motion of the heavens

---

[200] Nasr, *Science and Civilization*, 134.

is logically impossible.[201] Although al-Biruni himself thought that
the heavenly motions were circular, he scorned the notion that the
question could be settled without reference to observation. It was
eventually with the advantage of Tycho Brahe's extremely precise
observations centuries later that Kepler was able to show that the
planets did indeed move in elliptical, not circular, orbits.

> God is He who raised
> The heavens without any pillars
> That ye can see; is firmly
> Established on the
> Throne (of Authority);
> He has subjected the sun
> And the moon (to his Law)!
>   – Qur'an (13:2)

The Muslims' desire for a physical rather than purely mathematical model of the heavens introduced the "solidification" of
the heavenly spheres of Ptolemaic astronomy. In the *Almagest*,
Ptolemy treated the heavenly spheres as geometrical concepts. In
a later work called *Planetary Hypotheses* he sought to deal with
physical representations of the heavens using what was, in essence,
Aristotle's physics; these models, however, led to difficulties.[202] For
the Muslims, who took physics seriously, these difficulties were
unacceptable. In the next chapter we shall note the role played
by the solidification of the heavenly spheres in setting the stage for
the Copernican revolution.

The issue of whether the earth orbited the sun or the sun orbited
the earth was not theologically controversial for the Muslims, but it

---

[201] Nasr, *Science and Civilization*, 136.
[202] N. M. Swerdlow and O. Neugabauer, *Mathematical Astronomy in Copernicus's De Revolutionibus*. New York: Springer-Verlag, 1984, 44.

became controversial for Christian Europe. Muslim failure to adopt a sun-centered cosmology was not based on theological considerations. Al-Ghazali pointed out the irrelevance of the directions of physical space to the question of the location of God. He referred to the common practice of looking "up" to God as one of the "seventy thousand veils of light" that hides the true nature of God from human understanding. Al-Ghazali was insistent on the irrelevance of the shape of the universe to theology:

> ...[T]he fundamental question at issue between [the supporter of religion] and the philosophers is only whether the world is eternal or began in time. If its beginning in time is proved, it is all the same whether it is a round body or hexagonal figure; and whether the heavens and all that is below them form—as the philosophers say—thirteen layers, more or less. Investigation into these facts is no more relevant to metaphysics than an investigation into the number of layers of an onion or the number of seeds of a pomegranate, would be. What we are interested in is that the world is a product of God's creative action, whatever the manner of that action may be.[203]

Thus, there was neither physical nor theological reason to decide the issue of heliocentricity, at that time. Physical reasons to accept it would appear later, after the application of the telescope to astronomical observation. In the same way, there was neither physical nor theological reason to decide whether the earth rotated under fixed stars or whether the stars orbited around a stationary earth.[204]

---

[203] al-Ghazali, in Tahāfut, Kamali.

[204] Sarton (see George Sarton, *Introduction to the History of Science*) lists ʿAli ibn ʿUmar al-Katibi, Quṭb al-Din ash-Shirazi, and Abu-l-Faraj as astronomers who took special pains to prove that the earth was at rest and did not move in any way. Sarton notes that such efforts to disprove a point of view strongly suggest that there were others whom they were refuting.

Al-Biruni's *Kitab al-Hind* gives us insight into his overview of the question:

> As regards the resting of the earth, one of the elementary problems of astronomy, which offers many and great difficulties, this, too, is a dogma with the Hindu astronomers. Brahmagupta says in the *Brahmasiddhānta*: "Some people maintain that the first motion (from east to west) does not lie in the meridian, but belongs to the earth. But Var'hamihira refutes them by saying: 'If that were the case, a bird would not return to its nest as soon as it had flown away from it towards the west.'" And, in fact, it is precisely what Var'hamihirta says.

> Brahmagupta says in another place of the same book: "The followers of Aryanhata maintain that the earth is moving and the heavens resting. People have tried to refute them by saying that, if such were the case, stones and trees would fall from the earth."

> But Brahmagupta does not agree with them, and says that would not necessarily follow from their theory, apparently because he thought that all heavy things are attracted towards the center of the earth...

> Besides, the rotation of the earth does in no way impair the value of astronomy, as all appearances of an astronomical character can quite as well be explained according to this theory as to the other.[205] There are, however, other reasons which make it impossible. This question is most difficult to solve. The most prominent of both modern and ancient astronomers have deeply studied the question of the moving of the earth, and tried to refute it. We, too, have composed a book on the subject called *Miftāḫ `Ilm al-Hai'ah* (Key to

---

[205] Al-Biruni is addressing the issue of the rotation of the earth, but his arguments apply equally well to the question of motion around the sun.

Astronomy), in which we think we have surpassed our predecessors, if not in the words, at all events in the matter.[206]

Although the *Miftāh ʿIlm al-Hai'ah* (Key to Astronomy), appears to have been lost, it is clear that his reasoning was physical and not theological:

> It is the same whether you take it that the earth is in motion or the sky. In both cases it does not affect the astronomical sciences. It is just for the physicist to see if it is possible to refute it.[207]

Al-Biruni's faith in the harmony between the *tawhīd* revealed in the Qur'an and the *tawhīd* revealed by inductive research was so strong that he was ready to subject any matter to "merciless critique".[208] Thus, he indicted those Indian astronomers who allowed religious dogma to prevent them from looking too closely at religiously motivated theories that could not withstand inductive examination. Al-Biruni wrote in *al-Qānūn fi'l Tibb* that "the two points of view got mixed up in the course of time, and the discourse of astronomy was adversely affected."[209]

It is important to understand the implications of al-Biruni's assertion that the question of the earth's rotation is in need of resolution by physical considerations. Ptolemy had thought the issue was already settled on physical grounds. He conceded the point that rotation of the earth gives the same relative motion as a rotating heaven. Yet, he protested that it was "unnatural" that "the lightest and subtlest bodies either do not move at all or no differently from

[206] Edward C Sachau, *Alberuni's India*. New York: Norton & Co. Inc., 1971, 276-77.

[207] Al-Biruni (c. 1000), *Istīāb*. translated by S. H. Barani "Al-Biruni's Scientific Achievements," Indo-Iranica, 5 #4 (1952).

[208] Roger Arnaldez, "The Theory and Practice of Science According to ibn Sinā and Al-Bīrūnī," in *Al-Bīrūnī Commemorative Volume*, 428.

[209] See preceding reference.

those of a contrary nature".[210] Al-Biruni was certainly familiar with this passage in the *Almagest*, and obviously he did not find it persuasive. We have already pointed out that Al-Biruni rejected the presumption that the heavenly bodies were lighter than the earth on the grounds that there was no empirical evidence for this physical assertion. Something else, other than "lightness" may account for the fact that heavenly bodies remain above the earth.

Western historians of science who have not studied the Islamic scholars assume that because the Muslims never rejected the concept of a stationary earth, they were satisfied with Ptolemy's argument for rejecting it. However, this is clearly not the case for al-Biruni. His argument with Ibn Sina makes it clear that he thought the data that could resolve whether or not the heavenly bodies were heavy was lacking. He was insistent that science cannot be done without data. Al-Biruni's commitment to induction cannot be overstated. "Human reason needs data and no human being can be an exception from the need of Phenomena in which the mind functions," he wrote in his *Tahdīd Nihaya al-Amākin Li Tashih Masāfah al-Masākin* (completed in 1025 A.D.).[211] In the same work he criticizes those who "do not know the reality of the Qur'anic verse 'They ponder over the creation of the skies and the earth saying that the Creator has not created them meaningless.'"[212]

Ptolemy's physical reason for rejecting the rotation of the earth is that a stone thrown up in the air will fall back to its point of origin, not to a point "behind" it as he would expected if the earth moving. Yet, a number of Muslim scientists were unhappy with this answer, for different reasons.[213] Tusi [*d.* 1274] rejected this

---

[210] Claudius Ptolemy (c. 151), *The Almagest*. Bk. V, R. Catesby Taliaferro, trans., *Great Books of the Western World*. R. H Hutchins, ed., vol. 16, Chicago: Univ. of Chicago, 1952, 12.

[211] See Imad A. Ahmad, "Al-Biruni Commemorative Volume." (*review*), *Archeoastronomy*, vol. V #1 (Jan.-March 1982): 40.

[212] See previous note.

[213] Dallal, "The Astronomical Work of Sadr," 245.

argument on the grounds that concomitance of air and earth could account for the observation (consistent with Aristotelian physics). Qutb-ad-Din Shirazi [d. 1330] argued that even if earthly rotation is not natural, it could exist under compulsion. A force rotating the earth itself could be rotating the bodies on its surface as well.

The real response to Ptolemy's argument turns out to be momentum: The fact that a body in motion will tend to remain in motion. We must wonder whether, if al-Biruni had a better grasp of the concept of "momentum," he would have seen that it provides the physical solution to the problem of how planetary bodies counteract the force of gravity? That is, momentum causes the moon to orbit the earth without falling onto it, despite the fact that the moon is a heavy object. Similarly, the planets orbit the sun despite their weight, because their momentum offsets the acceleration of gravity towards the sun. The irony here is that it was the very man with whom al-Biruni was disputing this question, Ibn Sina, who was developing the concept of momentum at that time.[214]

John Philoponos had, in the sixth century, first rejected Aristotle's view that hurled objects continue moving because they are pushed by the air around them. He suggested that the bodies acquire an "impetus" in the act of being hurled that continues their motion temporarily, until the self-consuming impetus is used up. Ibn Sina considered that this impetus, or momentum, is not self-consuming, but permanent. Then, the only reason the hurled object slows down is the resistance to its motion offered by the air. An object in the vacuum of space could then continue to move forever.

Unfortunately, al-Biruni did not believe that outer space was a vacuum. That was demonstrated later by Ibn Mu'ādh (11th century), Mu'ayyid al-Din al-'Urdi (13th century), and Shirazi (14th century).[215]

---

[214] Aydin Sayili, "Ibn Sīnā and Buridan on the Motion of the Projectile," in *From Deferent to Equant*, 477-482.

[215] George Saliba, "The Height of the Atmosphere According to Mu'ayyad al- Dīn al-Urdi, Qutb al-Din al-Shīrāzī, and Ibn Mu'ādh." In *From Deferent to Equant*, 445-466.

Late in the eleventh century, Islamic Spain produced its first great observational astronomer. Az-Zarqali made an explicit proof of al-Battani's discovery of the motion of the earth-sun orbit. That is, he showed that the position of the sun against the background stars at the moment that it was farthest from the earth drifted gradually from one year to the next. His edition of astronomical tables known as the *Toledan Zij*, remained in wide use for centuries thereafter.[216]

Islamic astronomy became increasingly critical of the Ptolemaic's devices. Jabir Ibn Afla<u>h</u>, Avempace, Ibn Tufail, and al-Bitruji proposed or developed alternative theories, although none of these prevailed. "By the late medieval period, these violations" of physical or observational considerations were "sixteen in number and commonly referred to as *ishkālāt* (difficulties)...."[217]

In particular, Ibn al-Haytham wrote a treatise called *Ash-Shukūk `alā Batlamyās* (Doubts Concerning Ptolemy) which Swerdlow and Neugebauer characterize as "a rather ill-tempered diatribe against what he perceived to be errors, contradictions and impossibilities in the *Almagest*, the *Planetary Hypotheses*, and, rather briefly, the *Optics*." [218] Although some of Ibn al-Haytham's criticisms were rooted in "his own misunderstandings of Ptolemy's intentions," others "are right on the mark if Ptolemy's models are to be taken seriously as physical bodies in the heavens...."[219] Ptolemy's attempt to put his theory on a physical footing failed to live up to Ibn al-Haytham's standards. Ibn al-Haytham himself was unable to provide a replacement for Ptolemy's theory, although he did do some work on physical models to account for planetary latitudes.

---

[216] The Toledan Zij provide another example of the pluralism of Islamic society. Az-Zarqal joined a project initially commissioned by Sàid al Andalusi who patronized a large number of Muslim and Jewsih astronomers for the work. Sayili, *Observatory*, 181.

[217] F. Jamil Ragep, "The Two Versions of the <u>T</u>ūsī Couple." In *From Deferent to Equant,* 329-356.

[218] Swerdlow and Neugabauer, *Mathematical Astronomy,* 44.

[219] See previous note.

The last critical breakthrough came from the previously mentioned Maragha school of at-Tusi. The great thirteenth-century astronomer who produced precise measures of planetary motion showed that the motion of bodies in the solar system could be related to one another by spheres rolling within spheres, in effect a series of linked vectors. The model was developed and applied to various planets by his student Qutb al-Din ash-Shīrāzī and by the fourteenth-century astronomer, Ibn ash-Shatir. Ibn ash-Shatir emphasized that his objections to the validity of the Ptolemaic system were observational rather than philosophical. In his *Nihāyat as-Sūl fī Tashīh al-Usūl (The Final Quest Concerning the Rectification of Principles)* he wrote:

> Some of the verifiers of this science have enunciated some theoretical [*yaqīnīya*] doubts concerning those principles [i.e., Ptolemy's], while we enunciated other doubts that we based on observations [*waqafn'ā `alaihā bir-risd]* and the like.[220]

The Tusi couple had been invented to deal with latitude problems.[221] Although it had the happy side effect of eliminating Ptolemy's equant, this could hardly have justified the device since it introduced more epicycles than Ptolemy's system. Ibn ash-Shatir had only observational objections to Ptolemy's solar model, especially the size of the solar disk.[222]

Similarly, Ibn ash-Shatir relied on observations rather than philosophy to disprove the theory of trepidation mentioned in the preceding chapter. He refers to the observations as *haqīqa*, "the arbiters of truth."[223]

---

[220] George Saliba, "Theory and Observation in Islamic Astronomy: The Work of Ibn Al-Shātir of Damascus," *Journal History of Astronomy*, 18 (1987): 35.

[221] Saliba, History, 273. See also G. Saliba "Theory and Observation," 35-43.

[222] See previous note.

[223] See George Saliba, "Theory and Observation."

The tendency to want to look only at the data that supports our theories (or beliefs) is one of those human failings that scientists, and all seekers of truth, must try to overcome. The data that appears to violate one's theories provide the key to improving them, or overthrowing them in favor of better ones. Thus, the Islamic astronomers' concern over the "difficulties" of the Ptolemaic theory compared with Ptolemy's selectivity–Robert Newton would say fraud–in dealing with the data is significant.[224]

Unfortunately, Ibn ash-Shatir's discussion of the observational data upon which his model was based, the *Discourse on Observations* (*Ta'līq al-Arṣād*), appears to have been lost. The mere fact that it was ever written, however, shows the importance of observations to Islamic astronomers compared to their predecessors.

The other aspect of the Maragha school is their concern for the physics of planetary motion. Unlike earlier Muslim astronomers like the compilers of the *Toledan Zij*, these astronomers' primary concern was not deriving parameters but "with the physical problems of Ptolemy's models, particularly in the *Planetary Hypotheses*", and thus were attacking the kinds of issues previously raised by Ibn al-Haytham.[225]

E. S. Kennedy referred to at-Tusi's innovation as "the Tusi couple."[226] It can be imagined as a circle rolling within a larger rotating circle (or, imagine a rod connected by a pivot to another rotating rod and rotating around that pivot as well). Imagine that each circle (or rod) rotates at a certain speed. With an appropriate combination

---

[224] Modern science has gone one step further in the massive accumulation of data seeking confirmation or refutation of theories. On the other hand, modern scientists are not completely free of the bias towards excluding data that contradicts their views. See Thomas Kuhn, *The Structure* or, for a more humorous analysis, see Charles Fort, *The Book of the Damned*. New York: Holt, Reinhardt and Winston, 1941. This is why academic freedom is so important, so that the critical work of others can compensate for the shortcomings of each individual scholar's analyses.

[225] Swerdlow and Neugabauer, *Mathematical Astronomy*, 43.

[226] F. Jamil Ragep, "The Two Versions of the *Ṭūsī* Couple."

of circles (or rods) and speeds, one can model the motion of any planet. Copernicus' model was similar to that of at-Tusi and his school, but with the sun moved to the center and the circles rearranged accordingly.

To appreciate the similarity of Copernicus' model to that of at-Tusi's school, one should consider the model for the moon's orbit around the earth. Since there has never been a dispute about the fact that the moon orbits the earth, Copernicus' model of lunar motion is essentially identical to that of Ibn ash-Shatir. Ibn ash-Shatir drives the last nail into the coffin of the Ptolemaic model for the moon's orbit with an observational criticism: Ptolemy's model "requires that the diameter of the Moon should be twice as large at quadrature[227] than at the beginning, which is impossible, because it was not *seen* as such. [*lam yura kadhālika*]" (emphasis added by Saliba).[228] Further, Saliba argues that Ibn ash-Shatir's model for the motion of the sun must have been motivated by observational considerations *alone*, since he had no philosophical objection to the Ptolemaic solar theory.[229]

The naked eye observations that could distinguish between ibn ash-Shatir's model and Ptolemy's are the size of the moon as measured directly, the size of the sun as measured from eclipses, (e.g., whether solar eclipses are total, annular, or partial), and the "size" of the other planets as inferred from their brightness. Yes, the Muslim astronomers were aware of the effect of distance on brightness. Sadr, for example had argued that a planet would be "smaller" (i.e., fainter) during direct motion (when it is on the far side of its epicycle) than retrograde motion (when it is on the near side).[230]

---

[227] I.e. at the 1/4 and 3/4 point in its orbit.

[228] Saliba, "Theory and Observation."

[229] See previous note.

[230] Dallal, *Astronomical Work of Sadr*, 342.

The centers of astronomical activity had now moved to the edges of the Muslim world: Morocco, Persia and India. The last influential achievement of Islamic science would be Ulegh Beg's star catalog, the first new one since Ptolemy. At this stage in history the baton was passed on to Copernicus.

Figure 5

Ibn al-Haytham (at left) and Galileo on the frontispiece of Johannes
Hevelius' Selenographia (1647). (Frontispiece courtesy of
the Department of Printing and Graphic Arts, Houghton Library,
Harvard College Library, Typ 620.47.452F)

If indeed thou ask them Who has created the heavens and the earth
And subjected the sun and the moon (to His Law),
They will certainly reply, "God."
How are they then deluded away (from the truth)?
– Qur'an (29:61)

CHAPTER 6

THE IMPACT OF ISLAMIC ASTRONOMY ON THE WEST

He who is indifferent to the sciences and he who is asleep are ... of the same rank. – *al-Ghazali* [231]

S ome years ago, I had the opportunity to visit the Greenwich Observatory in England. There is a marvelous collection of astrolabes there. The astrolabe is a wonderful device that combines the functions of an analog computer, a star-map, and a sextant. It was named for the famed twelfth century manufacturer of scientific instruments al-Usterlabi. [232] Most of the astrolabes in the Greenwich Observatory display had what appeared to be Arabic writing on them. If one reads the plaques describing the exhibit, however, one learns that in many cases the writing was not authentic. European craftsmen would sometimes put Arabic writing on their astrolabes in order to give prospective buyers the impression that they were getting "the real thing" from the Muslim world. It would appear that, like the early days of transistor radios manufactured in Japan, consumers thought that the newcomers produced a product inferior to that of the people they were copying. The Europeans of the Renaissance, like the Japanese today, took the lead soon enough, however.

Islamic science passed to the West in stages. Mozarabs (Spanish Christians living in Islamic society) in tenth-century Iberian monasteries translated astronomical and mathematical works which passed into Europe "thanks to the active commercial route which, following the Rhone and the Rhine, reaches into the heart of Germany, and thanks also to the fact that the monk Gerbert, later Pope Sylvester II,

---

[231] al-Ghazali 1106-1111, *Ihya* I, 95.

[232] Sayili, *Observatory*, 176.

studied in Catalonia.[233] After a pause during the eleventh century brought on by Muslim trade sanctions (reacting to Christian translators who passed off the translated books as original works of Christian scholars), the translation movement regained full force in the twelfth century.[234] Texts translated were assimilated but not developed further until after the Renaissance. The last stage was the European acquisition of Islamic knowledge that followed the conquests of Spain and Sicily. Having acquired the universities there, the West acquired the knowledge contained therein.

From the beginning, an alleged conflict between science and religion was made an issue. As early as the 11th century, when European Christians first took up an interest in dynamics, they were confronted by critics who "maintained that explanations of these phenomena should be based on the biblical story of Genesis."[235]

Among the "hot topics" passed from the Islamic academies to the rising European ones was the issue of the motion of the planets. That issue was not theologically controversial for the Muslims but became controversial for the Christians. I have mentioned that the physical structure of the universe was irrelevant to Islamic theology, since God is transcendent and omnipresent. As we shall see, the physical structure of the universe was of significance to Christian theology because of the "Great Chain of Being" and its implications for the authority of the Church.[236]

---

[233] Juan Vernet, "Mathematics, Astronomy, Optics." In Joseph Schacht and C.E. Bosworth, eds., *The Legacy of Islam*. Oxford: Clarendon, 1974, 486.

[234] See previous note.

[235] Edgardo Marcorini, *The History of Science and Technology*, vol. 1. New York: Facts on File, 1988.

[236] Nasr, in *Science and Civilization* argues that the Great Chain of Being was essential to Medieval Islamic thought. Yet, the Qur'anic teaching that God's relationship to all Creation is direct contradicts the point of the Great Chain of Being, namely that God's connection to creation is hierarchical. The appearance of statements upon which Nasr bases his conclusion appears to me to be examples of the infiltration of medieval European Christian concepts. The Great Chain of Being aims at distancing the purely spiritual Creator from the material world, in contrast to the Qur'anic view that God "is nearer to him [Man] than (his) jugular vein"– Qur'an 50:16.

Ptolemy had dismissed the possibility of the earth's motion on the grounds that "in the light of what happens around us in the air," the mobility of a weighty earth and the immobility of the weightless sun and stars "would seem altogether absurd." We discussed in Chapter 5 how al-Biruni had argued that the weightlessness of the planetary bodies was unproven. The rejection of the assumption that the heavens and the earth were subject to two different sets of laws made the issue of what was at the center an open question from the physical point of view.

As described in Chapter 5, the mathematical model of the Maragha school permitted any body to be placed at the center of the system. Earlier scientists like Aristarchos of Samos (fl. c. 270 B.C., see Heath 1913) and Seleukos of Seleukia (second century B.C.?) had proposed heliocentric systems.[237] Van der Waerden has argued that the astronomical systems of the Indian scholar Aryabhata and of the ninth-century Muslim astrologer Abu Ma'shar al-Balkhi have the appearance of originally being heliocentric and reworked into geocentric form.[238] He points out, for example, that Abu Ma'sha's planetary revolutions "are heliocentric revolutions."

It is perhaps Al-Biruni's familiarity with Aryabhata that has led some Muslim writers to conclude that he was familiar with the heliocentric system.[239] Orientalists, on the other hand, are positive that no medieval Muslim astronomer was familiar with the heliocentric system. How anyone can be certain of either view given the apparent loss of the manuscript of the Miftāh`Ilm al-Hai'ah (Key to Astronomy) escapes me. The Syrian Christian astronomer Abu-l-Faraj went to the trouble of arguing against both rotation and rectilinear motion of the earth, raising the question as to whom he

---

[237] See Sir Thomas Heath, *Aristarchus of Samos*. Oxford: Oxford U. Press, 1913.

[238] B. L. van Der Waerden, "The Heliocentric System in Greek, Persian and Hindu Astronomy." in *From Deferent to Equant*, 525-47.

[239] See, e.g., René Taton, *History of Science*.

was arguing against.[240] The important point for our purposes is that the issue of the motion of earth, whether rotational motion which we know Al-Biruni did discuss, or orbital motion, was not theologically controversial for Muslims.[241]

The Polish astronomer Nicolaus Copernicus (1473-1543) owned a version of the Alfonsine Tables, which were a compilation of a variety of material, including both items from Ptolemy's *Handy Tables* and the *Toledan Zij*, initially put together in 13th-century Toledo under Alfonso X. Copernicus picked up where al-Biruni and at-Tusi left off. In fact, his model of lunar motion is the same as that of Ibn Ash-Shatir, although it was produced two centuries later. This has raised the question as to whether Copernicus was influenced by Ibn Ash-Shatir or the Marāgha school. Gingerich has expressed his doubts based on the absence of any Latin manuscript translating or describing Ibn ash-Shatir's work and the absence of any hard evidence that Copernicus saw the Greek translations of at-Tusi's work.[242] Others see it differently:

> The question is not whether, but when, where, and in what form he learned of Marāgha theory. There is evidence for transmission of some of this material, although how much is uncertain, to Italy in the fifteenth century by way of Byzantine sources....
>
> It is, however, certain that Tusi's device was known in Italy and applied to planetary theory, as shown by a curious treatise by one Giovanni Battista Amico [1536]....[243]

---

[240] See George Sarton, *Introduction to the History*.

[231] See Edward C Sachau, *Alberuni's India*. At least three other astronomers of the Islamic era also discussed this question; see George Sarton, *Introduction to the History*.

[242] Owen Gingerich, "Islamic Astronomy." *Scientific American*, vol. 254 #4 (April 1986): 74.

[243] Swerdlow and Neugabauer, *Mathematical Astronomy*, 47-48.

Amico was a strict Aristotelian who applied at-Tusi's device to concentric spheres with inclined axes. He was at the University of Padua. If he had learned of the Maragha school at Padua, why could not Copernicus, who spent 1501-1503 there? Copernicus need not have had access to Latin translations of the Maragha models. He may have had them explained to him by someone familiar with Greek sources.

Copernicus was able to apply the tools of At-Tusi's school to a hypothetical sun-centered system. In 1543, he published *De Revolutionibus Orbium Coelestium*, demonstrating that a heliocentric system was mathematically viable.

Copernicus' objection to Aristotle's view of gravity is reminiscent of Al-Biruni's. Alexandre Koyré remarked that it "contains an implicit negation of the concept of 'natural place,' which is the first step towards geometrization of space, one of the bases of modern physics."[244] But as we noted in Chapter 5, Al-Biruni had explicitly rejected the concept of natural place centuries earlier. Similarly, Koyré writes that Copernicus "asserts that the same laws apply to the heavens as to the Earth, and in so doing laid the basis of a profound change in human thought, to which history has given the name Copernican Revolution."[245] But this view, so revolutionary in the medieval European context, was, in the Islamic context, a mere restatement of the Qur'anic declaration that the unity of God is demonstrated by the unity of the laws governing His creation.

The objection has been raised that the fact that Copernicus retains the circular motions of planets suggests that he believed that such motions were "very distinct from terrestrial physics," undermining the implication that the laws of physics are universal.[246] Certainly, Copernicus accepted the naturalness of spherical

---

[244] Alexandre Koyré, *The Astronomical Revolution*. Paris: Hermann, 1973, 56.

[245] Alexandre Koyré, *The Astronomical Revolution*, 57.

[246] Owen Gingerich, private communication (1973).

motion and he was not offering a particular new theory of physics. Whether or not he himself felt such a theory was possible, a reader can understandably infer the possibility of such a theory from Copernicus' argument that gravity can explain not only sphericity of the earth, but that of the other planets as well. He considers gravity to be

> nothing more than a certain natural appetency implanted in the parts by the divine providence of the universal Artisan, in order that they should unite with one another in their oneness and wholeness and come together in the form of a globe. It is believable that this affect is present in the sun, moon, and the other bright planets and that through its efficacy they remain in the spherical figure in which they are visible, though they nevertheless accomplish their circular movements in different ways.[247]

Copernicus was arguing for the geometrization of nature, an idea he may have gotten from Nicholas of Cusa,[248] who was introduced to Islamic thought as a student at the University of Padua and eventually wrote *The Peace of Faith*, calling for inter-religious dialogue.[249]

The introduction to Copernicus' book, however, (generally believed to have been penned by Nuremburg's Lutheran pastor Andreas Osiander), obscures any revolutionary implications by professing that the book presents a mathematical hypothesis. This was politically wise. The Church reacted strongly against the idea

---

[247] Nicholaus Copernicus 1543, *Revolutions of Heavenly Spheres* I, ix. *trans.* Charles Glenn Wallis, *Great Books of the Western World*, vol. 16, 521. The fact that different sets of epicycles described the motions of different planets no more precluded a universal theory of physics to account for those motions than the fact that the ellipses Kepler later used to describe the planetary motions had a different eccentricity for each planet which precluded Newton from developing the theory of universal gravitation to account for those orbits.

[248] Koyré, *The Astronomical Revolution*, 113.

[249] Roger A. Johnson, "The Beginnings of a Modern Theology of Religions: Nicholas of Cusa (1401-1464)." Boston Theological Institute Faculty Colloquium (12/5/02), http://www.bostontheological.org/colloquium/bts/rj.pdf (accessed 8/29/03).

that this model was to be understood physically, because it would overthrow the Great Chain of Being.

In the Middle Ages, European Christians viewed all existence as a "Great Chain of Being," which we mentioned above. Their cosmology provided a material structure in which this great chain resided. They viewed God, the Exalted, as literally "on high" in a celestial realm at the borders of space. Below Him were the celestial spheres of the angels and below that the spheres of the planets, then the earth.

The Christian version of this marriage of theology and cosmology provided a rationale for the Church's powerful position in society. God was at the top of this chain and the archangels next (etc.) down to the Pope and then the cardinals (etc.) and then the parish priest and then the masses. It is unknown whether the presentation of the Copernican model as a hypothesis reflected doubts as to physical reality of the heliocentric model, or a fear of Church reaction to a paradigm that destroyed the theological case for the Church's authoritarian hierarchy.[250] The sensitivity of the issue is unambiguously demonstrated by the fate of Giordano Bruno.

Bruno was a sixteenth-century Italian philosopher, influenced by the works of Ibn Rushd. He was forced to flee from charges of heresy in Italy and ended up in England giving lectures on the Copernican theory at Oxford. After attacking Aristotelianism there, he fled again to Frankfurt. He was invited to Venice but the Inquisition extradited him to Rome where he was burned at the stake for heresy.

Bruno went beyond the side issue of whether the sun or the earth was at the center of the universe and directly to the question of whether the universe had a center at all. The significance of

---

[250] Martin Luther called Copernicus a "Narr" (the German word for fool, see Swerdlow and Neugebauer, *Mathematical Astronomy*). Copernicus' theory was not taught in the Polish Protestant schools until 1722 and in the Catholic schools until 1782. See Bunkowska, Barbara. "From Negation to Acceptance." in *The Reception of Copernicus' Heliocentric Theory*. Dordrecht: D. Reidel, 1972.

Bruno's insight and his debt to the Islamic legacy with which he made contact at Padua is summarized in these excerpts from Singer's biography of Bruno:

> ... [B]oth critics and followers of Copernicus in the six-teenth century saw in his work a rearrangement of the well-established world scheme.... to Bruno and Bruno alone the suggestion of Copernicus entered into the pattern of a completely new cosmological order. In this sense Bruno not only anticipated Galileo and Kepler, but he passed beyond them into an entirely new world....
>
> The whole of Bruno's philosophy is based on his view of an infinite universe with an infinity of worlds. He conceived the universe as a vast interrelationship throughout space and time....

Some ancient thinkers had glimpses of this vision as had later thinkers, Moslem, Jewish and Christian. Their thought was not unknown to Bruno.

> The infinity of time and space had been rejected by ortho-dox Christian thought in medieval Europe, but was more or less cautiously set forth in a whole body of Moslem and Jewish writings which were translated into Latin between the twelfth and fifteenth centuries. These conceptions were widely canvassed in the universities of North Italy and France and especially in Padua and Paris.[251]

Bruno refers to Avicenna, Avicebron, Solomon Ibn Gabrial, Averroes and Nicolaus of Cusa (*d.* 1464).[252] The University of

---

[251] Dorothea Waley Singer, *Giordano Bruno: His Life and Thought*. New York: Greenwood Press, 1950, 50-53.

[252] A European Christian who was very familiar with Islamic literature.

Padua had no religious tests for students or professors. "The contrast between the modern bias toward observation and the scholastic interest in ratiocination had declared itself at Padua."[253] Bruno's attitude, shocking to the Church, finds no quarrel in Islam. The Qur'anic verses "Praise be to God, the Lord and Cherisher of the Worlds" (1:2) and "He is the Lord of Sirius (the Mighty Star)" (53:49) harmonize with Bruno's rhapsody:

> This is the excellence of God magnified and the greatness of His kingdom made manifest; he is glorified not in one, but in countless suns; not in a single earth, but in a thousand, I say, in an infinity of worlds.[254]

Although some Muslim philosophers under the influence of Western philosophy (e.g., ibn Sina) incorporated the neoplatonic chain of being into their philosophy,[255] their theology was not accepted by the mainstream *ulama* (scholars) and was refuted by al-Ghazali,[256] Al-Ghazali did not deny that the universe was shaped like an onion, he only insisted that if it were indeed shaped like an onion, such was the will of God and not a logical necessity. That is, he rejected the notion that "it could have been no other way," as Aristotle would say. Al-Ghazali is absolutely clear that he believes that the universe might have been shaped in any of a wide variety of ways, and that the actual shape is a choice made by the Almighty, the product of God's will. Thus, the claim that a heliocentric theory would constitute a "metaphysical transition" that "forced an intellectual breach with traditional Islamic cosmology"[257] is a case of misreading Western theology into Islamic theology.

---

[253] Singer, *Giordano Bruno*, 54.

[254] Giordano Bruno 1584, *De'l Infinito Universo e Mondi in Dorothea*. Waley Singer, Giordano Bruno.

[255] See Ian Netton, *Allah Transcendent: Studies in the Structure and Semiotics of Islamic Philosophy, Theology and Cosmology.* (Richmond, Surrey: Curzon Press, 1989).

[256] See the quote on p. 102.

[257] Huff, *Rise*, pp. 59-60.

For orthodox Islam, God is both transcendent and immanent. The Medieval Church saw these as mutually exclusive; thus, the necessity for the incarnate "Son" who would bridge the gap between transcendent God and fallen Man. Bruno's views challenged both the Great Chain of Being and the Platonic dichotomy of the divine versus the material at its root. The challenge cost him his life.[258]

Galileo Galilei (1564-1642) was an Italian astronomer who also argued for the Copernican viewpoint. Galileo was a major contributor to the development of experimental methods in Europe. Although we have no evidence that Galileo was directly influenced by Muslim thought, he remembered Bruno's fate and he recanted his position that the earth moves.[259]

Galileo actually looked at the signs of God in the heavens to see if they indicated whether the earth or sun was at the center of planetary motion. He went beyond his Muslim predecessors by using a telescope to investigate more closely the physical appearances of the heavenly bodies. He made a number of discoveries that could be interpreted to support the Copernican model. But one discovery in particular was definitive: Galileo found that Venus went through phases, as the moon does. In the case of Venus, however, the phases showed that it sometimes was on the opposite side of the sun from the earth. Thus, Venus did not go around the earth but must

---

[258] Although some Muslim philosophers under the influence of Western philosophy (e.g., ibn Sina) incorporated the neoplatonic chain of being into their philosophy (see Ian Netton, *Allah Trancendent:* theology was not accepted by the mainstream *ulama* and was refuted by al-Ghazali. Thus, the claim that a heliocentric theory would consituted a "metaphysical transition" that "forced an intellectual breach with traditional Islamic cosmology" (Huff, *Rise*, 59-60) is a case of misreading Western theology into Islamic theology.

[259] J. Brownoski, *The Ascent of Man.* (Boston: Little, Brown, 1973) 214, 216 says that Bruno was shown the instruments of torture. Owen Gingerich (private communication, 2003) doubts that Galileo was actually shown the instruments and believes the reference to torture in the Inquisition's file on Galileo (which we saw during a visit to the Vatican archives) "was simply a legal expression indicating how hard they could press him, but someone Galileo's age would probably not actually be shown the instruments of torture."

be going around the sun![260] The same turns out to be true for Mercury. Then, every planet (except the moon, no longer deemed a planet but a mere satellite of the earth) might be considered to go around the sun. Galileo initially reported his discovery of the phases of Venus to Kepler in a doubly coded message. This was a way of insuring the priority of his discovery a few months before he was certain of its revolutionary significance.[261]

Earlier, we noted the Muslims' belief in the relevance of physics to astronomy and how this was manifested in the idea that the heavenly spheres had some sort of physical reality. Now that the telescope revealed that Venus, at least, went around the sun, the idea of solid spheres was no longer tenable, for Venus would smash the sun's sphere in the course of passing through it. While, mathematically, it still made no difference whether the earth went around the sun or the sun around the earth, the physical basis for the geocentric system had been destroyed.

The critics of Galileo's telescopic observations had cause to question their reliability. They were familiar with carnival mirrors that distorted reality. The optical quality of Galileo's telescopes was more like that of toy telescopes one can buy today than modern research telescopes. It was just as proper for the Church to question Galileo's authority for his scientific conclusions as it was for Galileo to question the Church's authority. The attitude of "Question authority!" is an appropriate–even necessary–one for

---

[260] "Observations of Venus and the sun led ... [ninth-century] astronomers [of the Baghdad and Damascus observatories] to adopt a non-Ptolemaic model which, according to Nallino, was tantamount to 'transforming the orbit of Venus into an epicycle whose constant centre was the real position of the sun.' Unfortunately, the Arabs failed to conclude that Venus was a satellite of the sun." Taton, *History of Science*, 409-410.

[261] "The Jesuits at the Collegio Romano in Rome had a telescope and verified his claims. The reason Galileo issued the Venus phases anagram was that he feared the Jesuits might scoop him, and he wanted a means to establish his priority." Owen Gingerich (private communication, 2003).

scientific progress. The problem is that the Church was not simply questioning Galileo's research–they were attempting to suppress it. Galileo could defend against challenges to the value of his equipment for the purposes to which it was put by demonstrating the repeatability and consistency of his observations or by experimental research aimed at any particular objection. But he was not allowed to make his case. There was a political issue at stake: The Church did not want its authority subject to question.

Galileo sought to establish his right to defend the Copernican system on the grounds that the "Holy Spirit intended to teach us in the Bible how to go to Heaven and not how the heavens go."[262] This was putting a new spin on St. Augustine's warning "we do not read in the Gospel that the Lord said: I will send you the Paraclete to teach you how the Sun and the Moon move. Because he wished to make them Christians, not mathematicians!"[263]

The argument was ineffective, for the Church's political authority was married to the "Great Chain of Being." The Church's chief theologian, Cardinal Robert Bellarmine, feared that Catholicism might be undermined in its fight with Protestantism. On Feb. 26, 1616, bearing a letter from the Pope, he ordered Galileo "in the name of His Holiness the Pope and the whole Congregation of the Holy Office, to

---

[262] Galileo Galiei 1614, "Letter to the Grand Duchess Christine of Lorraine," quoted by Henry Crew and Alfonso de Salvio in *Biographical Note in Great Books of the Western World*, vol. 28. Galileo himself was quoting the Vatican librarian Cardinal Boranius.

[263] De Actis cum Felice Manichaeo, I.2. "As is emphasised by both Fantoli A. *Galileo: For Copernicanism and the Church* (Notre Dame: Notre Dame Univ. Press 1996), 14 and R. J. Blackwell, *Science, Religion and Authority: Lessons from the Galileo Affair* (Marquette, Wisconsin: Marquette University Press, 1998), 15-16. This is largely because Augustine does not think science is very important. What matters to him is salvation, and science is only significant if it obstructs that—as when Christians bring scandal on the faith by opining on subjects of which they know nothing." Stephen May, "The Galileo Affair or How NOT to Engage in the Theology/Science Debate," Symposium on Science and Christianity to honour Harold Turner and John Morton, Auckland Apr. 21, 2001. http://www.spc.org.nz/2.pdf (accessed 8/27/03).

relinquish altogether the opinion that the sun is the centre of the world and immovable, and that the earth moves, nor henceforth to hold, teach, or defend it in any way whatsoever, verbally or in writing." Within a few weeks of this order, the Congregation of the Index placed Copernicus' book on the index of prohibited works.

Galileo had been tactless. By putting the Pope's views into the mouth of a character named "Simplico" in his *Dialogue on the Two World Systems*, he was provoking the religious establishment. While many hailed the book as a "literary and philosophical masterpiece," the Jesuits

> charged that the book could have worse consequences "than Luther and Calvin put together." The Pope, in anger, ordered a prosecution.... [A]t that point a document was "discovered" in the file, to the effect that during his audience with Bellarmine ... Galileo had been specifically enjoined from "teaching or discussing Copernicanism in any way," under penalties of the Holy Office.[264]

Thus, we can discern the political motivations behind the persecution that led to Galileo's recanting. The mystical-authoritarian structure we discussed in Chapter 2 bears its fruits. From this incident in Western history, the myth of a conflict between religion and science draws its nourishment.

It was Galileo's contemporary, Kepler, who found that placing the sun at (or, more precisely, near) the center removed the need for epicycles, equants or deferents. Instead, a purely elliptical orbit would account even for Tycho Brahe's very precise observations. The planets moved in simple ellipses, quickly when near the sun and more slowly when further away. Isaac Newton was then able to provide the physical basis for this motion which Aristotle thought

---

[264] Giorgio de Santillana, "Galileo," in the *Encyclopaedia Britannica, Macropaedia,* vol. 7. Chicago: Encyclopaedia Britannica, Inc., 1980.

impossible: universal gravity offset by conserved momentum. Al-Biruni's hypothesis that all bodies are subject to gravity and Ibn Sina's conviction that momentum is conserved were vindicated at last.

Kepler's achievement is an important one, for his model features both of the elements that one who believes in a universe designed by God expects to find: a model as inherently beautiful as the hypothesis of circular motions *and* a strict quantitative accounting of the observations. Thus, Kepler is in the tradition of Ibn al-Haytham and has transcended the dichotomy of St. Thomas Aquinas conventionalist theory of science.[265] Aquinas had argued that there are two ways of inducing scientific systems:

> One way is for proving some principle as natural in science where sufficient reason can be brought to show that the motions of the heavens are always of uniform velocity. In the other way, reasons may be adduced which do not sufficiently prove the principle, but which may show the effects which follow agree with that principle, as in astronomy a system of eccentrics and epicycles is to be accounted for. But this is not a sufficient proof; because possibly another hypothesis might also be able to account for them.[266]

Now that theoretical beauty and quantitative precision had *both* been satisfied, all that remained missing was a physical basis to the theory. That would be provided by Newton.

The fourteenth-century European scholar Jean Buridan discussed the conservation of momentum in terms that paralleled Ibn

---

[265] Michael Polanyi, *Personal Knowledge: Towards a Post-critical Philosophy*. Chicago: Univ. of Chicago, 146.

[266] St. Thomas Aquinas 1269, *Summa Theoligica*, Part 1, ques. 32, quoted in Polanyi, *Personal Knowledge*, 146.

Sina.[267] Galileo started out with the belief that momentum was self-consuming, but by the end of his career, after numerous experiments in mechanics, he converted to Buridan's (i.e., Ibn Sina's) view. Newton's first law of motion is a quantification of this principle that an object in motion will remain in uniform motion unless acted upon by an outside force.

The Church had defined the alternatives: faith or science, and literally forced the people to a choice. The scientists had demonstrated that they could prove their theories. Europe revolted against the anti-science of the Church. The Church had not simply sided with an outmoded physics, it had sided with an outmoded theory of knowledge. Galileo could not "demonstrate" the motion of the earth as necessary consequence of self-evident axioms and so the Church banned not only his provocative exposition of the Copernican hypothesis, but Copernicus' own tactful presentation as a "mathematical hypothesis." But Ibn Haytham and Galileo had changed the way science was done since the ancient Greek times. They had produced a "demonstration" not by simple deduction from axioms but by consistent accurate prediction. Al-Ghazali, who had advocated this new theory of knowledge centuries before Galileo had warned that if you force people to choose between science and "faith" they would choose inductive science.

He who thinks that it is his religious duty to disbelieve such things [as proven astronomical theories] is really unjust to religion, and weakens its cause. For these things have been

---

[267] Again, the question as to whether the European groundbreakers were influenced by the Islamic heritage arises. Sayili (see Aydin Sayili, "Ibn Sinā and Buridan") has examined the reasonableness of the claim that Buridan was influenced by Ibn Sina. Eurocentric scholars may object that the evidence is purely circumstantial. There are innumerable examples of Renaissance scholars whose ideas parallel Islamic developments. Ultimately, we are reminded of Henry David Thoreau's dictum: "Some circumstantial evidence is very strong, as when you find a trout in the milk" (quoted in Bernard Darwin, *The Oxford Dictionary*). I think that one must concede, at the very least, an indirect influence.

established by astronomical and mathematical evidence
which leaves no room for doubt. If you tell a man who has
studied such things–so that he has sifted all the data relating
to them, and is, therefore, in a position to forecast when a
lunar or solar eclipse will take place: whether it will be total
or partial; and how long it will last–that these things are
contrary to religion, your assertion will shake his faith
in religion, not in these things. Greater harm is done to
religion by an immethodical helper than by an enemy whose
actions, however hostile, are yet regular. For, as the proverb
goes, a wise enemy is better than an ignorant friend.[268]

Galileo tried to have it both ways. Before the Inquisition, he
repudiated his conviction in the motion of the earth, but no one
today believes that he really changed his mind. He continued doing
his scientific research and wrote *Discourse on the Two New
Sciences*, which he had smuggled to Leyden for publication and
which was immediately denounced by the Church and placed on
the index of forbidden books.

The West was eager to embrace the science rooted in the Islamic
heritage, but did not want to embrace the Islamic religion. The legacy
of the Crusades had made such a prospect unthinkable. Few
Westerners had any idea of what the Islamic religion was, anyway.
They imagined it to be just a foreign brand of blind faith in some
different but equally unpalatable dogma.[269] The West fractured ideo-
logically, as different groups chose different paths for reacting to the
challenge.

The Protestant Reformation tried to reconcile science and religion by reforming religion, in the process adopting a number of

---

[268] al-Ghazali 1106-1111, *Tāhāfūt*, Kamali.

[269] See, for example, Thomas Paine's *The Age of Reason* in which he uses arguments reminiscent of those in the Qur'an to argue for the existence of God and then presents arguments
against Christian dogma as arguments against religion in general.

Islamic concepts. The Bible was published and made available to the masses. The priesthood was replaced by a more democratic ministry. Bathing, which at one time could be used to bring you before the Inquisition, was no longer suspect and the new motto became "cleanliness is next to Godliness."

It was in Protestant England that scientists like Isaac Newton found support for the new science "in Reformation ideas of the sovereignty of God and the total dependency of matter. Newton himself was convinced that nature demonstrated the existence and activity of God, but not the Trinitarian God of orthodox Christianity."[270] When John Locke expressed an interest in publishing Newton's religious ideas, Newton declined. Fearing the reaction to his opposition to Trinitarianism, Newton was unwilling to question religious authority in print.[271] Newton's religious views were perfectly orthodox with regard to the doctrines central to Islam, however. His own summary, found in the *General Scholium*, with which he concludes the Principia, makes clear that he espouses neither pantheism nor deism but a theism, which in Islamic circles would classify him as a *hanīf*, the title given to Abraham for attaining a certainty in the uniqueness of God's divinity from his examination of nature (see Chapter 2).

> This most beautiful system of the sun, planets, and comets, could only proceed from the counsel and dominion of an intelligent and powerful Being. And if the fixed stars are the centers of other like systems, these, being formed by the like wise counsel, must all be subject to the dominion of One....

---

[270] See David C. Lindberg and Ronald L. Numbers, *God and Nature*.

[271] Richard S. Westfall, "The Rise of Science and the Decline of Orthodox Christianity: A Study of Kepler, Descartes, and Newton." in David C. Lindberg and Ronald L. Numbers, *God and Nature*. 230.

> This Being governs all things, not as the soul of the world, but as Lord over all; and on account of his dominion he is wont to be called *Lord God* ... and *Deity* is dominion of God not over his own body, as those who fancy God to be the soul of the world, but over servants. The Supreme God is a Being eternal, infinite, absolutely perfect.... He is eternal and infinite, omnipotent and omniscient; that is his duration reaches from eternity to eternity; his presence from infinity to infinity; he governs all things, and knows all things that are or can be done.... We adore him as his servants....[272]

These sentiments are as acceptable to Christians as they are to Muslims. The source of Newton's fear of persecution lay in his conviction that "fraud had entered the Bible."[273] Newton's letters to Locke on "Notable Corruptions of Scripture" were founded on evidence he had collected that

> the passages on which Trinitarians had relied had been inserted into the Bible in the fourth and fifth centuries.... The corruption of Scripture stemmed from a corruption of doctrine, primarily the work of Athanasius ... who denied the original and true form of Christianity represented by Arius... In the end, every aspect of Christianity was involved in the lapse from truth, from the ecclesiastical structure on the one hand to the moral tone of society on the other. Although he did not say so directly, Newton clearly believed that the Protestant Reformation had only scratched the surface. It had left the source of infection, Trinitarianism, untouched.

---

[272] Isaac Newton 1687, *Mathematical Principles of Natural Philosophy*. Andrew Motte, Revised by Florian Cajori, in *Great Books*, v. 34, 369-370.

[273] Richard S. Westfall, "The Rise of Science."

... With the later deists, he shared a hatred, which stood at the very heart of his Arianism, of mystery and superstition. Trinitarianism was built on superstition in his view. Athanasius had deliberately contrived it for the easy conversion of heathens "by bringing into it as much of the heathen superstition as the name of Christianity would then bear...."

For Newton, who carried further the tendency present in Kepler and Descartes, Nature was the revelation of God as much as the Bible was, perhaps more so....[274]

The continuing attachment of mainstream Protestants to the fundamental problematical notion in Christianity, the Trinity, placed them in opposition to Newtonian Christianity and left them an easy target for the critics of religion in the modern era. Historian Margaret Jacob (1986) has traced the development of the reaction of what she calls "the Tory or 'country' wing of the Anglican church" against the Newtonians and the liberal Anglicans who were perceived as soft on "science-supported natural theology."[275] In a universe that mechanically obeys fixed laws, they saw, not the hand of God, but an undermining of religion in general. This reactionary movement "also displayed strongly mystical and spiritualizing tendencies. It sought to keep aspects of Newtonian science, while finding in nature proof for doctrines as diverse as the Fall of Man and Trinity." For them, materialists were the "wayward, but inevitable, offspring of their science-deceived elders. Even within Cambridge itself a reaction set in against the alliance of science and religion."[275]

---

[274] See previous note.

[275] Jacob, Margaret C. 1986, "Christianity and the Newtonian Worldview." in David C. Lindberg and Ronald L. Numbers, *God and Nature*, 250.

Jacob gives the example of George Cheyne (1671-1743), an early convert to Newtonian natural philosophy, who subsequently abandoned it "and opted for an increasingly spiritualized understanding of nature and for a contemplative, almost mystical and millenarian version of Christianity.... For the first time in Protestant Europe, the eighteenth century witnessed a widespread disaffection from the new science...."[276]

A counter-reaction ensued on the other side, which articulated itself in the defiantly anti-religious climate of the French Revolution, with Jacques André Naigeon's argument that "soon God would be exposed as an excess wheel in the mechanism of the world." It culminated in Laplace's pointed remark in the 1813 edition of the *Exposition du Système du Monde* that "I cannot forego noting here how Newton strayed on this from the method that he otherwise used so effectively."[277]

Out of this background, we find in the nineteenth century, scholars like Draper and White making blanket statements about warfare between science and religion.[278] Yet, an examination of Draper's cases shows that his real target is the Catholic Church.

Other religious bodies receive little but praise. Islamic scholars, he claimed, laid the foundations of several sciences; the Greek Orthodox church had generally welcomed science; Protestants had cultivated a "cordial union," marred only by occasional "misunderstandings." In fact, Draper regarded the Protestant Reformation, with its insistence on the private interpretation of Scripture, as the "twin sister" of modern science.

---

[276] Jacob, "Christianity," 251.

[277] Hahn, Roger 1986, "Laplace and the Mechanistic Universe." in David C. Lindberg and Ronald L. Numbers, *God and Nature.*

[278] John William Draper, *A History of the Intellectual Development of Europe.* And Dickson White, *A History of the Warfare of Science with Theology in Christendom.*

Thus, we have seen how, out of the complex interaction within European society, brought on by the Church's attempt to preserve its authority against a paradigm-shift triggered by the introduction of Islamic science into Europe, the myth of the conflict of religion and science was born. Extreme rationalists have lumped all religion into the camp of anti-science. This certainly is unjustified, even if one is only speaking about Christianity. Fairness (not to mention a scientific attitude) requires that one note the differences between the various denominations lumped together. The Unitarians rejected Trinitarianism, but kept the name of "Christians." The Friends (Quakers) rejected all creeds and adopted their own version of Ibn Tufail's concept of the "Inward Light."[279] Deists retained a belief in the existence of God, but avoided disputes over dogma by dismissing any concept of worship. Among the Fundamentalists, those who argue the Bible is both inerrant and literal, have sided with blind faith against science.

Since the nineteenth century, it is the issue of "Creationism" that has done the most to keep the myth of the war between science and religion alive. Consider the argument that scientific data is not conclusive because God may have planted misleading evidence. Some Fundamentalists have suggested that God has created artifacts with a carbon-date billions of years old in a universe that is less than ten thousands years old. Muslims, however, do not generally attribute practical jokes to God. Or, as Einstein more elegantly put it: "Subtle is the Lord, but malicious He is not."[280]

Einstein, the archetype of the modern scientist, did not believe that there was any inherent antagonism between religion and science. "All religions, arts and sciences are branches of the same tree," he wrote. "All these aspirations are directed toward ennobling man's life, lifting it from the sphere of mere physical existence and

---

[279] See Nasr, *Science and Civilization*, 316.

[280] Abraham Pais, *"Subtle Is the Lord—": the Science and the Life of Albert Einstein.* New Brunswick, NJ: Transaction Books, 1982.

leading the individual toward freedom."[281] He understood that the techniques of natural science yield a different sort of knowledge than the techniques of religious contemplation. Thus, he said it is "clear that knowledge of what is does not open the door directly to knowledge of what *should be*."[282] Such conflicts as did arise he attributed to that characteristic prominent in Fundamentalism. This term is most often used to refer to those who hold the Bible to be inerrant and literal. Einstein asserted that

> a conflict arises when a religious community insists on the absolute truthfulness of all statements recorded in the Bible. This means an intervention on the part of religion into the sphere of science; this is where the struggle of the Church against the doctrines of Galileo and Darwin belongs. On the other hand, representatives of science have often made an attempt to arrive at fundamental judgments with respect to values and ends on the basis of scientific method, and in this way have set themselves in opposition to religion. These conflicts have all sprung from fatal errors.[283]

The essence of Einstein's religiosity was his belief in a non-anthropomorphic God.[284] God is manifested in the orderliness of the universe, not in a human shape. The tendency of humans to seek to depict God as a human being is one of those fatal errors to which Einstein referred. One might say that in Islamic thought, this particular sort of fundamentalism is the root error of all errors, an example of *shirk*, associating partners to God, the gravest sin.

---

[281] Albert Einstein, *Out of My Later Years*. New York: Philosophical Library, 1950, 9.

[282] Albert Einstein, *Later Years*, 22.

[283] Albert Einstein, *Later Years*, 25-26.

[284] R. Buckminster Fuller, "Einstein." in *Cosmography: A Posthumous Scenario for the Future of Humanity*. New York: Macmillan, 1992, 76.

I would like to note here that, despite the press' incessant use of the term "fundamentalist" to describe some Muslims, the word is misleading. It only serves to confuse conservative or traditionalist Muslims with extremists or fanatics. There can be no distinction among Muslims analogous to the modern Christian movement known as "Fundamentalism." The term is most often used to refer to those Christians who hold the Bible to be inerrant and literal. *Every* Muslim believes the Qur'an is *inerrant* and *no* Muslim believes it is always *literal*. The former would contradict the Qur'an's claim of authorship by God, and the latter would contradict its assertion that it is in part allegorical:

> He it is Who has sent down
> To thee the Book:
> In it are verses
> Basic or fundamental
> (Of established meaning);
> They are the foundation
> Of the Book: others
> Are allegorical. But those
> In whose hearts is perversity follow
> The part thereof that is allegorical,
> Seeking discord, and searching
> For its hidden meanings,
> But no one knows
> Its hidden meanings except God.
> And those who are firmly grounded
> In knowledge say: "We believe
> In the Book; the whole of it
> Is from our Lord:" and none
> Will grasp the Message
> Except men of understanding.
>
> – Qur'an (3:7)

Despite the agreement between the Qur'an and Einstein on the dangers of literalism, I do not discern in Einstein's writings on religion an Islamic essence such as Newton expresses. Einstein does not merely object to Biblical literalism, he denies the possibility of objective knowledge of ethics completely: "Objective knowledge provides us with powerful instruments for the achievements of certain ends, but the ultimate goal itself and the longing to reach it must come from another source."[285] Further, he attributes the source of such historical conflicts between religion and science to the belief in a personal God: "In their struggle for the ethical good, teachers of religion must have the stature to give up the doctrine of a personal God, that is, give up that source of fear and hope which in the past placed such vast power in the hands of priests."[286] This argument only applies to a religion that denies a direct relationship between God and the individual. Any religion that, like Islam, insists that each individual is *directly* responsible to God has the opposite effect–it frees the individual from submission to any intermediary.

To the degree that Einstein is rejecting an anthropomorphic concept of God, he is in agreement with Islamic thought. However, Einstein goes beyond this and objects to prayer on grounds reminiscent of Frazer's analysis of the subject discussed in Chapter 2.[287] Einstein rejects the idea that God answers prayers or would reveal an objectively verifiable code of life to mankind. His concept of God as One who has strictly determined everything in the universe (who does not "play dice") leaves room neither for the miraculous nor for the free will of mankind. Einstein explicitly states that he finds a belief in free will (or equivalently in Divine reward and punishment) as contradictory to

---

[285] Albert Einstein, *Later Years*, 22.

[286] Albert Einstein, *Later Years*, 28-29.

[287] Albert Einstein, *Later Years*, 26-28.

God's omnipotence. It is Einstein who seems to be guilty of a contradiction here. If God is omnipotent, then why does Einstein deny His power to create free will or quantum uncertainties? And if God permits no departure from strict determinism (not even to mankind), then why does Einstein concern himself with ethics (with what *should be*) at all? It does not seem to have occurred to him that God might *choose* to grant humans some (limited) freedom of will. Evidently, he finds such a notion to be inconceivable, as he found quantum mechanics incredible. But that is another book. I would only note here that the paradoxical relationship between free will and determinism is a source of frustration to theists and atheists alike.

The difficulties posed by a personal God who rewards and punishes creatures of His own design are less troublesome than those of an impersonal God who leaves His creatures to the consequences of their actions without any mercy. Perhaps it is the lack of emphasis on God's attribute of mercy in the Old Testament of Einstein's Jewish background that has permitted him to overlook this point. The Qur'an stresses God's mercy more than any other attribute. The fact that the literally anthropomorphized God of the New Testament is formulated around the attribute of mercy shows the fallacy of concluding that the concept of a personal God necessarily implies that creatures shall be punished for faulty design by their Maker. As Umar Khayyam put it:

... Some there are who tell
Of One who will toss to Hell
The luckless Pots He marr'd in the making–Pish
He's a Good Fellow and 'twill all be well![288]

Einstein had little familiarity with Islam. Although he is taken as the archetype of the modern scientist, I can attest that my scientific colleagues have a wide range of religious views–similar to that

---

[288] *Rubāiyāt of Omar Khayyām* trans. by Edward Fitzgerald.

found in the general population. "The argument from design" still has its advocates in the scientific community.[289] We have seen that the myth of the conflict between religion and science actually arose from a *political* conflict in Western history when scientific knowledge passed on from the Islamic world and challenged the theology of a politically powerful Church. It was this event that created not only the myth of a war between science and religion, but precipitated the demand for Church/State separation. In the next chapter we shall look at a science/religion controversy current in the Muslim world and see evidence of political causes there as well.

---

[289] See, e.g., Paul Davies, *The Mind of God: The Scientific Basis for a Rational World.* New York: Simon and Schuster, 1992.

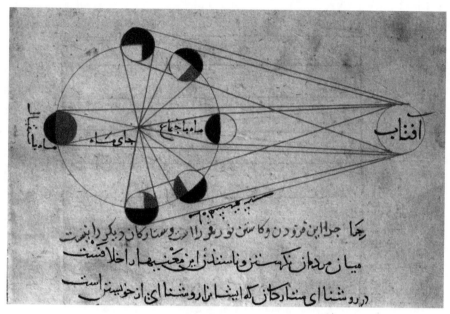

Figure 6

Diagram by al-Biruni of Phases of the Moon
from *Kitāb al-Tafhīm* (by Roland Michaud from Nasr 1976)

They ask thee concerning the New Moons.
Say: They are but signs to mark fixed periods of time
In (the affairs of) men, and for Pilgrimage. . . .
– Qur'an (2:189)

CHAPTER 7

THE LUNAR CALENDAR PROBLEM[290]

> Prophets and religious leaders of necessity made mankind
> have recourse to independent judgment, even though they
> might fall into error. – *al-Ghazali*[291]

T he only way the term "fundamentalist" might reasonably be
applied to some segment of the Islamic movement is to
apply it to those who wish to return to the fundamental
teachings of the Qur'an. That message, we have seen, is pro-science
and pro-tolerance. Such a use would be the reverse of the intent of
those who use the word as a pejorative against the Islamic resurgence. Yet, the European colonization of the Muslim world has
infected many Muslims with this fallacy of an antagonism between
faith and science. The leading Islamists know better, and the
Islamic resurgence is strongest among the well-educated Muslims,
but the myth is still strong among the masses and impedes the
resurgence of Islam.

One of the most challenging problems of classical astronomy is
the determination of the time when the new moon crescent can first
be seen. A study of this problem provides insight into both Islamic
science and juridical matters. It also gives some insight into the sad
political state of modern Muslims.

The Islamic community in the early 21st century bears little
resemblance to that of the golden era discussed in previous chapters,

---

[290] Revisions in the second edition include material from my paper "The Rise and Fall of
Islamic Science: The Calendar as a Case Study, " delivered at the conference on "Faith and
Reason: Convergence and Complementarity" at al-Akhawayn University, Ifrane, Morocco
June 3, 2002.

[291] Watt, *The Faith and Practice of Al-Ghazzâlî.*

either educationally or politically. In that sense, an analysis of the new moon crescent and the calendar problem it poses is a good prelude to a discussion of the reasons for the decline of Muslim civilization and the prospects for an Islamic renaissance. The obstacles that have inhibited the resolution of that problem represent the obstacles to the progress of science in the Muslim world.

The Islamic calendar is very simple in principle. Each day begins at sunset. There are twelve months of the year. The new moon marks the beginning of each new month. Then why all the confusion among Muslims on how to read this clock God has placed in the sky–especially at the beginning and end of Ramadan (the Muslim month of fasting)?

The Muslim religious calendar is a strictly lunar calendar. Traditionally all dates are based on a twelve-month year with the beginning of each month calibrated to sightability of the new moon crescent. Such a calendar will have a year of 354 or 355 days. The pre-Islamic Arabic calendar had been a luni-solar calendar. It was also calibrated by sighting of the new crescent, but occasional leap months were inserted in order to keep the calendar in sync with a solar year of approximately 365.25 days.

The problem with the pre-Islamic calendar was that there are four sacred months under which warfare is prohibited. The decision whether or not to insert a leap month in a particular year could alter the months during which fighting was permitted. The pagan Arabs had allowed military considerations to be the determining factor in when they would insert the leap months. This practice was prohibited in the Qur'an and, as a result, intercalation was banned by the Muslims, leaving the strict lunar calendar.

One might think that the prohibition of intercalation would cause a serious problem for the Muslims, for example in areas like agriculture. How can a farmer know when to plant his crops when his calendar is divorced from the seasonal cycle? In fact, the prohibition only resulted in an incentive for the development of more sophisticated tools for the tracing of dates. The simple calendars that suffice to determine planting and harvest times in the solar calendar are inadequate to the task in the Muslim year that slides against the seasons. Thus, one of the first Muslim scientific accomplishments was the printing of tables predicting the probable weather conditions from the climatic impact of the earth's position in its orbit, much as their descendent *The Old Farmers' Almanac* does today. (As previously noted, the word "almanac" comes from the Arabic *al-manākh* which means climate.) These almanacs were the beginning of Islamic science.

The real challenge for the Islamic calendar was not the absence of intercalation, which really only simplified the problem, but rather the difficulty of predicting when the new moon could be seen. Figure 6 shows how the moon moves around the earth with respect to the sun. When it lines up between the earth and sun that is an *astronomical new moon* (astronomical *conjunction*). At that time, the moon cannot be seen from earth because it is too close to the sun. It is too close to the sun to be seen for a variety of reasons. For one thing, it is lost in the glare of the daylight scattered from the sun by the air. *It is not until many hours later that the new moon can be seen.* Primarily, the lit side of the moon is then facing the sun, away from the earth. The moon will not be visible until it sets after the sky has become dark enough for the moon's faint light to exceed that of the background sky. Determining that time is one of the most complex problems of classical astronomy.

To some degree this problem had been solved by pre-Islamic astronomers, and the Muslims learned of those solutions from the translation movement and further refined the techniques.[292] In the 8th century Yaqub ibn Tariq produced tables for calculating sightability

---

[292] Mohammad Ilyas, *Astronomy of Islamic Calendar*. Kuala Lampur: A. S. Noordeen, 1997.

and Habash developed a calculation system. In the 9th century al-Khwarizmi devised a method for predicting visibility based on the "arc of light" or the elongation of the moon from the sun. In the same century al-Battani and al-Farghani developed refinements to the ancient methods of using the time of moonset after sunset in the special case where the arc of light was large. Many others, (including non-Muslims working in the Muslim civilization like Thabit ibn Qurrah and Moses Maimonedes), followed.

To engage in such refinements one needs more than mathematics and rational analysis. One needs reliable reports of the earlier work on which one is building and empirical data on which to build the refinements. As we have shown, Muslims dedicated themselves to such efforts employing all three factors of attaining knowledge and benefited from the seven factors encouraging Islamic science, outlined in Chapter 3.

It takes the moon 29-1/2 days to travel around the orbit, as illustrated in Figure 6. Thus, the month may be 29 or 30 days. The Prophet warned his companions that they were an unlettered people who could "neither read nor count," and that they must therefore prefer to sight the moon rather than calculate its position–although if the day were cloudy, they could calculate it by waiting 30 days from the previous new moon.[293] Later, when Islamic civilization flourished, the Muslims could do more than count and write. As we have seen, they had invented spherical trigonometry. The scholars were able to calculate the approximate time when a new moon could be sighted. Today, we can calculate the exact time of the *astronomical new moon* as well.

When sighting was more reliable than calculation, the community was told to rely on sighting. Today, calculation is more reliable than sighting. This has raised the question to what degree Muslims should now rely on calculation? Shall we follow the superficial, perhaps temporary, meaning of the hadith (visual sighting) and ignore its principal, eternal, meaning (be accurate)?

[293] Abdul Hamid Siddiqi, *Sahīh Muslim*, ch. CDVI 2376, 2378.

There are four sources of confusion:

(1) Disagreement whether the new moon must be sighted (or at least visible) on the first day of the month, or if it is sufficient that it exists as defined by astronomers.

(2) Disagreement whether the moon's visibility (or existence) is to be determined locally (a day for each community) or globally (one day for the whole world).

(3) Disagreement whether reported sightings should be accepted automatically or only when they are scientifically reasonable.

(4) Failure of organizations entrusted with the duty of implementing one system or another to follow their own professed system.

Unfortunately, it is the last of these that has caused the most problems. I say "unfortunately" because the other three sources of confusion are more easily resolved. I believe that most Muslims would gladly abandon their adherence to one side or another of the first three questions for the sake of unity, but are frustrated from doing so by doubts that any system they commit to will be followed by other Muslims.

Rather than long for a priestly authority to dictate a global resolution to this confusion, Muslims would be well-advised to take a scientific approach. If some local communities consistently followed a simple scientifically sound system for meeting the religious requirements for a local calendar found in the sources of Islamic law, such a system might be expected to spread by emulation. Unfortunately, rather than consistently follow a scientific system for determining the calendar dates, Muslims have attempted to take advantage of modern high-speed communications to follow the dates observed, for example, in the Gulf states. They appear to be unaware that a calendar date valid in Saudi Arabia, say, may be not be valid in Texas. At the same time, most modern states in the Muslim world lack the environment of free speech under which academic debate could expose the flaws in their own calendrical systems.

As a prelude to the next chapter, I shall first show why the Islamic calendar problem is solvable by scientific methods and then I shall give an example of how modern Muslims' departure from these methods sustains the continuing confusion.

Muslims take the Qur'an for guidance in this as in all other matters. There are two requirements of the Islamic calendar in the Qur'an. The first is that the calendar must be tied to the lunar cycle:

> They ask thee concerning the New Moons.
> Say: They are but signs to mark fixed periods of time
> In (the affairs of) men, and for Pilgrimage....
> > – Qur'an (2:189)

Second, the number of months in the year are twelve:

> The number of months in the sight of God
> Is twelve (in a year)–so ordained by Him
> The day He created the heavens and the earth;
> Of them four are sacred; that is the straight usage....
> > – Qur'an (9:36)

Finally, the calendar must be consistent and not tampered with for political purposes:

> Verily the transposing (of a prohibited month)
> Is an addition to Unbelief: The Unbelievers are led
> To wrong thereby; for they make
> It lawful one year, and forbidden another year,
> In order to adjust the number
> Of months forbidden by God
> And make such forbidden ones lawful....
> > – Qur'an (9:37)

The Qur'an, then, requires that the calendar be of months of FIXED LENGTH, determined by the NEW MOON, CONSISTENT, and with 12 MONTHS IN THE YEAR.

The moon's orbit around the earth with respect to the sun (the month) takes slightly more than 29-1/2 days. Thus, the lunar calendar month must be of 29 or 30 days in an irregular alternation. It takes the earth more than 12 months of 29 or 30 days to go around the sun. Thus, the Islamic calendar will become a little earlier each year measured against the solar calendar in common use (the Gregorian calendar).

These requirements are clear and simple but they are not sufficient by themselves to resolve the issues causing the confusion. Thus, we turn to the jurists' understanding of the *sharī'ah* (Islamic law) and to science.

The jurists are agreed that the month must begin if a sighting has been achieved or if 30 days have passed since the beginning of the previous month. Thus, knowing that the moon has been seen (because of sighting) or can be seen (because of the passage of thirty days) requires marking the new month. According to most scholars, it does not matter whether the moon has been sighted from a different location. Those who admit a nonlocal sighting, however, require that the sighting must be made before dawn in all places to which it would apply. Their reasoning is that *one must know with certainty whether to fast before dawn* so that proper intention may be made. This means that a person in a place where the moon cannot be seen may accept that a new month has begun because he is certain that a person in another place has seen the moon. Although not all jurists have required that an actual sighting of the moon be made, they hold that the moon must at least be *sightable*, i.e., apart from such considerations as weather. Some hold that the relaxed criterion of sightability only applies to 30-day months, while others believe that it could be applied to a 29-day month where uncontested astronomical calculation guarantees sightability.

The Lunar Calendar Conference held in Herndon, Virginia in June, 1987 resulted in a unanimous statement of the participating astronomers. That unanimous statement declares certain points on which there is *no scientific disagreement*. The entire statement can be found in the conference proceedings.[294] The points with a direct bearing on the sources of confusion are summarized below:

(1) For each lunar month, a curved band may be drawn on the surface of the earth, west of which the new crescent must be visible on a certain day, east of which the new crescent cannot be seen on that day but will definitely be seen on the next day (local weather conditions permitting) and inside of which observation is difficult and reports must be carefully examined for reliability and consistency with the scientific facts.

(2) No matter what basis is used for the Islamic calendar, conventions for a global calendar are unavoidable.

(3) Contradictions between countries using calculations are due to the fact that they are calculating different things. If the *fuquha* (Islamic jurists) provide a uniform definition of what they want calculated, this sort of contradiction should not occur.

We shall shortly see that the key point to resolving the problems lies in point (2), that conventions are unavoidable. A convention is a rule adopted for convenience. For example, during the winter in northern Canada the sun never sets. When shall a Muslim there pray Maghrib, `Isha', and Fajr (sunset, dusk, and dawn, respectively) prayers? Some scholars have recommended that they follow the nearest populated area with "normal" prayer times. But what is a "normal" prayer time? However it is defined, the prayer time would be a matter of convenience and therefore a *convention*.

The fact that the adoption of conventions is unavoidable provides the key to reconciling the conflicting requirements discussed above. To prove this, let us look at a few systems in current use:

---

[294] Imad-ad-Dean Ahmad, ed. *Proceedings of the IIIT Lunar Calendar Conference*, 2nd ed. Herndon: IIIT, 1998.

(1) The Malaysian system: The month begins if astronomical conjunction (the moon's change from old to new) occurs before the moon sets. This is the simplest system given the availability of precise calculations of the time of astronomical conjunction. To make it work at high latitudes, one need only define the effective time of the new day in the absence of a sunset. To make it a GLOBAL system, however, one would have to adopt a convention that the entire world would date the new month based on astronomical conjunction at a particular place.

(2) The Egyptian system: The month begins if the moon sets a certain time after sunset. This is a very simple system, but will not work at high latitudes. There, in addition to the problem noted with the Malaysian system, the moon may not even be above the horizon for days. One could make it global by a convention that uses some latitude at which the moon is above the horizon for at least some part of every day of the year.

(3) The Moving Lunar Dateline (MLD): This is the system proposed by Muhammad Ilyas and adopted (but not strictly followed) by the Islamic Society of North America (ISNA). The MLD is the "band" referred to in point number (1) of the unanimous statement of the astronomers summarized above. This system requires a number of conventions to be applied at high latitudes. The details are too complicated to discuss here.[295]

(4) The Saudi system: The new month begins when a new crescent is sighted whether or not such a sighting is theoretically possible. This is the simplest system in the absence of calculations (though highly unreliable). It is completely useless as a local system at high latitudes. To make it a global system would require letting places at high latitudes rely on observations at other locations, arbitrarily selected.

---

[295] Readers who are interested should refer to Ilyas, *Astronomy of Islamic Calendar*.

In a pamphlet written for the lay Muslim,[296] I explained a set of conventions that would provide a system that meets all the *fiqh* (Islamic jurisprudence) and scientific requirements, yet would be uniform for the Western hemisphere:

(1) That the new moon must be born before sunset in Mecca.

(2) That the new crescent must be sightable somewhere in the world on the first day of the lunar month.

(3) That, for the Americas, a part of the night must be shared with the place of first sighting.

This is not the place to discuss the merits of my proposal as opposed to that of any other (for example that of Ilyas 1984). The purpose of this discussion has been to establish that the religious requirements can be addressed in a scientific manner. (Readers interested in the details are referred to my pamphlet.) What is of interest here is that the problem remains unresolved. Many Muslims refuse to even read scientific discussions of the question, confusing the calculation of probable times of sighting with astrology. An astronomer in a Muslim country asked me not to openly discuss a letter he sent in reference to the subject because of the "sensitivity" of the issue.

I myself have been affected by the absence of academic freedom in the Muslim world today. In 1987, I chaired a scientific conference on the Islamic calendar. As editor of conference proceedings, I took great care to make sure that all the papers were in satisfactory final form. When they were published, I was stunned to find that *my own paper* was filled with typographical errors, including my own name misspelled in the byline. I compared the printed version against the camera-ready copy I had submitted and discovered that my paper had been entirely retyped, evidently by someone unskilled in English, for the sole purpose of deleting one sentence: "This year, Saudi Arabia began its fast before the commencement of the new moon by any scientifically acceptable definition." My efforts to

---

[296] Imad-ad-Dean Ahmad. *A Uniform Ilamic Calendar for the Western Hemisphere (1411 A.H.-1413 A.H.).* Bethesda: Imad-ad-Dean, Inc., 1990.

determine who deleted this sentence and whether they acted on their own were met by advice that the issue is "sensitive." The fear of questioning authority prominent in Galileo's era, discernible in Newton's reluctance to publish his challenges to Trinitarianism, is glaringly evident in the Muslim world today.

The role of the seven factors in Islam mentioned above in the development of the lunar calendar are self-evident. The question is then how has the falling away from these factors affected the calendar problem in Muslim society today?

There are certain parts of the Muslim world, for example in Pakistan, where actual sightings are attempted by the masses, guided by astronomical calculations of the most likely times of sightability. Most American Muslims, however, simply call relatives in their home countries and accept hearsay reports that some unidentified person has seen the moon somewhere. In Saudi Arabia, large cash awards offered for the first sighting, with no restrictions based on astronomical theory, have resulted in a situation in which one of a handful of people from the same locations repeatedly claim the award almost invariably on sightings impossible according to astronomical theory and often on dates preceding the physical occurrence of the astronomical new moon.[297]

Rather than induction, today's Muslims employ an extremely crude empiricism. Attempts by Muslim astronomers to explain why the crescent cannot be sighted before the new moon are rebuffed by the masses on the grounds that the "Western" defined new moon is not an Islamically defined concept—ignoring it is a simple universal fact that a new crescent cannot be seen before an astronomical new moon is not simply a matter of definition. The failure of the Muslim community to question the Saudi establishment's acceptance of impossible sightings bestows a quasi-priestly sanction to

---

[297] Salman Shaikh, "Hilaal Sighting in Saudi Arabia & Its Implications Worldwide," talk given at Islamic Society of North America meeting on the Lunar Calendar in Indianapolis, IN, Nov. 2000.

the role of the Saudi government. Of course, the absence of academic freedom is a contributing factor to that failure. The reliance on hearsay demonstrates the degree to which proper citation has fallen out of favor. The fact that there are so few Muslim astronomers and that the ones who exist are so ignored attests to the collapse in the emphasis on learning and study.

Lack of material success plays no role in this matter. The Muslims have the material resources to solve this problem. Not only have they not elected to use their vast material resources to produce, for example, an orbiting lunar observatory that could conclusively resolve all doubts about moonsighting (while at the same time bringing forth a rebirth of eminence in astronomy), they have not even expended the mere thousands of dollars it would take to produce a reliable 100-year calendar of Islamic dates based on any of the scientifically valid models advocated by a variety of Muslim astronomers. A contributing factor to this failure may be the anemia of free markets in the Muslim world, but that cannot account for the failure of, for example, American Muslims to fill the gap.

The failure of the Muslim world to settle the calendar problem without the recurrent feuding that attends this issue is a reflection of a lack of respect for science among modern Muslims. I believe that previous chapters have made clear that such a lack of respect does not come from the fundamental principles of Islam. Rather, it is a symptom of a departure from those principles, which we have discussed. The dispute over the Islamic calendar does not have the fundamental implications for theology that modern planetary theory had for the Great Chain of Being. Nonetheless, both science and religion are impacted by the absence of the political freedom in the Muslim world. As we shall argue in Chapter 9, any renaissance of Islamic science will require a return to the fundamental Islamic principles that sparked the original Islamic scientific civilization.

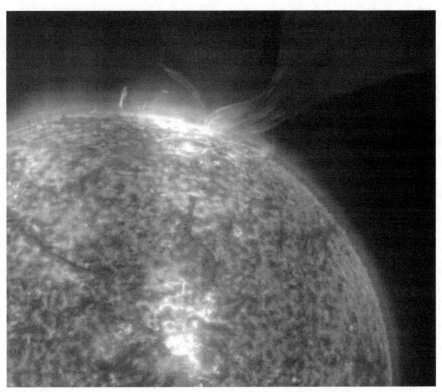

Figure 7
Matter Escaping from the Sun
(NASA)

Among His Signs are the Night and the Day
And the Sun and the Moon.
Adore not the sun and the moon,
But adore God, Who created them,
If it is Him ye wish to serve.
– Qur'an (41:37)

CHAPTER 8

THE INCOHERENCE OF MUSLIM PSEUDOSCIENCE

[The study of astronomy] has no bearing on metaphysical investigation. For this is as if someone were to say that the knowledge that this house came to be through the work of a knowing, willing, living builder, endowed with power, requires that one knows that the house is either a hexagon or an octagon and that one knows the number of its supporting frames and the number of its bricks, which is raving, its falsity obvious; or that one does not know that this onion is temporally originated unless one knows the number of its seeds–[all] of which is abandonment of [rational] discourse, discredited by every rational person. – *al-Ghazali* [298]

Despite the fall of Muslims from their pre-eminent position in the sciences to the sad state in which they find themselves today (the reasons for which will be discussed in the next chapter), almost no Muslims have turned against science. Yet, there are among the Muslims, literalists who, while sincerely believing themselves to be enthusiasts of science, are laying the groundwork for an anti-science backlash by repeating the mistake of the medieval Church, i.e., marrying their interpretation of scripture to current scientific theory. Should the day come that any of these theories are disproved, their intellectual heirs shall turn against the science of the future and declare it to be a heresy against "scripture." This phenomenon is worth some discussion because its practitioners have adopted the term "Islamic science" for their

---

[298] al-Ghazali c. 1095, *Incoherence*, 2000, 8-9.

practice, even though it is not science and, insofar as it ignores the Qur'an's warning against confusing allegory with basic facts (3:7, quoted under Figure 7 in front of this chapter), it is not Islamic.

"Islamization" of knowledge has meant many different things to different people. The most visible area of activity has been the development of so-called Islamic banking. A wide variety of venture capital investments, joint development projects, and partnership financing have been developed to avoid the appearance of charging interest. There have been no serious efforts however to "Islamize" the natural sciences. Instead, the works of the late physician Maurice Buccaille have inspired a wave of bad imitators seeking, in effect, to demonstrate that the Qur'an is a scientific textbook. This development has earned the scorn of real scientists like Pervez Hoodbhoy who, unfortunately, accepts the label of "Islamic science" for the Islamic pseudoscience he attacks.[299] By this confusion of terms, he asserts that the "Islamic science" of the classical era should simply be called "Muslim science" (i.e., science that happens to have been done by Muslims) and thus ends up denying the religiously inspired elements of scientific methodology that we have discussed in this book

In his best-selling book, *The Bible, the Qur'an, and Science,* Buccaille argued both that the Qur'an had a greater internal consistency than the Bible and that the metaphors of the Bible become quainter with the advancement of scientific knowledge, while the metaphors in the Qur'an have become more meaningful. Despite the fact that he found the way certain phrases in the Qur'an acquired the appearance of allusions to recent scientific discoveries to be a miraculous testimony to the Book's Divine origin, Buccaille nonetheless correctly insisted that the Qur'an is not a scientific textbook. He never suggested that one could *derive* scientific knowledge from

---

[299] Pervez Hoodbhoy, *Islam and Science:Religious Orthodoxy and the Battle for Rationality.* Atlantic Highlands, N.J.: Zed Books, 1991.

analysis of the Qur'an. Yet, Bucaille's imitators have argued that the theory of special relativity, and even the precise speed of light can be deduced from the Qur'an.

To understand the subtle but extremely important difference between Bucaille's claims and those of the pseudoscientists, let us contrast two of Bucaille's claims against two of the imitators. Bucaille claims that a Qur'anic phrase that refers to the manufacture of milk in cattle posed a challenge for medieval scholars to understand.

> And verily in cattle (too) will ye find an instructive Sign. From what is within their bodies between excretions and blood We produce for your drink milk pure and agreeable to those who drink it."
>
> – Qur'an (16:66)

Based on the medieval knowledge of the anatomy of cattle the claim that milk comes from "between excretions and blood" can only be considered baffling. As a physician who lived after the discovery of the details of the digestive process, however, Bucaille easily reads "between excretions and blood" to mean "coming from the conjunction between the contents of the intestine and the blood,"[300] a poetic reference to the scientific fact discovered in modern times that nutritional substances of the body are collected by the bloodstream from chemical transformations taking place along the interface to the digestive tract from the partially digested matter in the intestine, passing through the intestinal wall. Of course, this was completely unknown to Muhammad, who could not even have known of the circulation of the blood, which was not discovered until more than four centuries later.[301]

Living in a time when Edwin Hubble's discovery of the expansion of the universe is well known to all educated people, Bucaille is quick to see it in the phrase on the Creation of the universe:

---

[300] Bucaille, *Bible*, 209.

[301] See p. 76.

> With power and skill did We construct the Firmament [lit.: the sky]: for it is We Who create the vastness of space [lit.: Who are expanding it].
>
> – Qur'an (51:47)

Notice how Yusuf Ali, translating the verse shortly before Hubble's great discovery, avoids the literal meaning. No doubt, he found it unintelligible. Bucaille embraces the literal meaning, which conforms to an expanding universe, but he never suggests that one could have deduced that the universe is expanding from the verse. This reflects an emphasis on the Qur'an as a book of guidance, rather than as a book of science. A verse that could have been interpreted as alluding to the vastness of space may now be understood as referring to the expansion of space, yet the point of the verse was, is, and always will be, that space, whatever its nature, is the creation of the Almighty and its nature is determined by His will.

Now contrast this approach to that of the practitioners of Muslim pseudoscience. For them this verse doesn't allude to the expanding universe, but predicts it. It is as if the Qur'an were a scientific text, the careful reading of which would "teach" us the nature of the universe. In exactly this manner, Dr. Mansour Hassab-Elnaby in a paper entitled "A New Astronomical Qur'anic Method for the Determination of the Greatest Speed C"[302] claims that his interpretation of verses 22:47 and 32:5 demonstrates "the validity of the special theory of relativity."[302] This claim falls short both on grounds of scientific methodology and on religio-epistemological grounds from which al-Ghazali attacked the metaphysical claims of the philosophers.

It is true that verse 22:47 can be translated, "A day in the sight of thy Lord is like a thousand years of your reckoning," and surely

---

[302] Mansour Hassab-Elnaby, "A New Astronomical Qur'anic Method for the Determination of the Greatest Speed C," (5/1/01) http://www.themodernreligion.com/science/speed-c.html (accessed 8/29/03).

this is an assertion of the relativity of time. But it is an assertion of the relativity of *psychological* time, not of the *physical* time of a body in motion as predicted by the special theory of relativity. That a day of time to the omnipotent Creator of the Universe would seem like us as a thousand years is to be expected when we compare our finite capacity for comprehension to His infinite Mind. Indeed, a thousand years would seem to be a rhetorical understatement. Rather one should say that an instant in the site of God is as an eternity in our time. Why insist that this sentiment must be interpreted as miraculous prediction of the discovery of relativity and not accord the same status to the identical statement in the Bible?[303]

Elnaby's calculation of the speed of light relied on a different verse, "God rules the cosmic affair from the heavens to the earth. Then this affair travels, to Him (i.e., through the whole universe) in one day, where the measure is one thousand years of your reckoning" (32:5).[304] Elnaby uses a complicated method of doing this calculation in order to, he says, remove the effects of general relativity from the result. If Elnaby had simply shown that his hypothetical interpretation yields a number in agreement with the speed of light, he would have appended another provocative factoid to the Bucaille canon. But he didn't stop there, he states that his analysis validates the special theory of relativity, as if the theory would have been put in question if he had gotten a different number. But the fact is that the verse does not say that the "the cosmic affair" travels at the speed of light, nor does it give a distance that it must travel.

Since "your reckoning" for Muslims means the lunar calendar, Elnaby interprets "one thousand years of your reckoning" to mean the distance traveled by the moon in a thousand lunar years of its orbit around the earth. His interpretation is attractive only because of his claim that the numbers work out. Otherwise, alternative interpre-

---

[303] 2 Peter 3:8.

[304] I use Elnaby's translation here, which seems closer to the Arabic than Yusuf Ali's.

tations would have been more attractive. For example, the "day" which is a thousand years of our reckoning could easily have been the Day of Judgment, which to our human perception seems like a thousand years. Even if the verse really is a reference to the theory of relativity, it could have been interpreted as a reference to time dilation, say to the fact that the "cosmic affair" travels at a speed such that in its inertial reference frame a day seems like a thousand years.

I will not here address the question of whether the numbers actually do work out. In fact, there are serious technical questions about the analysis that would have been raised if the paper had been submitted for peer review. (Pseudoscience does not undergo peer review.) Even if the numbers did work, there are other problems.

The real difficulty is not the suggestion that God sent Muhammad the speed of light in code the way Galileo sent Kepler his observation of the phases of Venus in code.[305] It is the claim that this interpretation somehow "validates" the special theory of relativity. Should Muslims take this claim seriously, they will set themselves up to turn a scientific theory about the nature of the universe into an article of religious dogma. Muslims must not marry the spiritual guidance of the Qur'an to a specific theory, like the theory of special relativity lest they set themselves up to persecute any scientist who questions that theory as Galileo was persecuted. A theory about the physical universe stands or falls on its power to help us understand the universe and its success in doing so. An interpretation of a verse of scripture stands or falls on its ability to bring us closer to the Divine and into submission with His Will.

Another danger to such an approach is that it misrepresents science as a body of facts instead of the process that it is. The approach to science manifested by these pseudoscientists draws on the educational system now dominant in the Muslim world in

---

[305] See p. 127.

which knowledge in general is a body of facts to be memorized rather than a human construction that attempts to bring all known facts into a coherent whole. The real Islamic contribution to science, as this book has attempted to show, is the role it played in bringing about the methodology that marks modern science. The "facts" of science that the Muslims of the classical era discovered have often been superceded by newer discoveries, just as the "facts" embraced by scientists of the eighteenth century have been replaced by those embraced by scientists of the twentieth century. The "modern" approach to knowledge, which was the approach of the early generations of Muslim scholars, is to *critically* examine the coherent structure offered by the previous generations of scholars with the intention of understanding it, questioning it, reforming it, or, if necessary, replacing it completely. This is the essence of *ijtihād*.

The incoherent approach of the Muslim pseudoscientists suffers from the flaws that al-Ghazali criticized in the philosophers. The philosophers too sought to rationalize the "self-evident" axioms of previous philosophers into harmony with the scientific theories popular in their own day, and argued that the latter followed with logical inevitability from the former. Today's Muslim pseudoscientists take the powerful symbols of holy text, give them a literal interpretation that can be rationalized into harmony with the scientific theories popular today, and argue that the latter follow with logical inevitability from the former.

The claim that the Qur'an contains scientific facts in such a way that it "predicts" the discoveries of modern science has turned "Islamic science" into a sad joke.[306] By making the phrase "Islamic science" disreputable, it has given more power to those who claim there is nothing worthwhile in Islam over those who know better. Thus, an encyclopedia that was in fact devoted to the

---

[306] "All scientific ideas must be shown to be consistent with, if not derived from, the Sharî a." Huff, *Rise*, 235.

history of Islamic science was instead given the name "Encyclopaedia of the History of Arabic Science" and an exhibition on Islamic medicine was named "Medicine in the Age of Caliphs."[307]

Modern science is not a body of facts. It is a *process* for the study of the nature world. Because of human fallibility, that process yields a constantly changing set of conclusions about *how* this world operates. The Qur'an is an unchanging statement about *why* we are here. Confuting the very different disciplines of religion and science can only work to the detriment of both.

---

[307] David A. King, "Proposal for an Exhibition on Islamic Science and Technology," submitted to UNESCO 1997. http://www.unesco.org/pao/exhib/islam2.htm (accessed 8/30/03).

Figure 8
Drawing from Flammarion (1888).
(Courtesy Owen Gingerich)

... But those in whose hearts is perversity
Follow the part thereof that is allegorical,
Seeking discord and searching for its hidden meanings,
But no one knows its hidden meanings except God.
And those who are firmly grounded in knowledge say:
"We believe in the Book; The whole of it is from our Lord";
and none will grasp the Message except men of understanding.

– Qur'an (3:7)

CHAPTER 9

PROSPECTS FOR AN ISLAMIC RENAISSANCE

In the latter days there will be ignorant worshipers and sinning learned men. *–al-Ghazali*[308]

The Golden Era of Islam lies far behind us. Today, Muslim scientists of Nobel Prize winning stature are the exception, not the rule. Rather than engage in research unraveling the ways in which God operates the physical universe, Muslims engage in games seeking hidden meanings in the Qur'an that accord with the scientific discoveries of non-Muslims. This can be associated with the "closing of the door to *ijtihād*" by the Muslim establishment. *Ijtihād*, one of the sources of Islamic jurisprudence, comes from the same root as *jihād*, or holy struggle, and refers to the scholar's struggle for correct understanding. By the time of Islam's fall to the West, in the fifteenth century, *ijtihād* had been replaced by *taqlīd* (unquestioning imitation) throughout most of the Muslim world.

While we have shown that it is an exaggeration to claim that Islam did not give birth to modern science,[309] it is fair to ask why did the evolution of science in Islam reach the point of establishing the methods of modern science and then stop? Why did Muslim science peak in the twelfth century, at the time of al-Biruni? Although it continued to burn bright for a time in varying areas of

---

[308] al-Ghazali, *Ihya*, vol. 1, 71.

[309] See, e.g., Huff, *Rise*, p. 47.

the Muslim world, eventually these parts of the Islamic domain fell to the rising European tide. The West picked up the torch of knowledge and the Muslim world retreated into darkness.

There is no general agreement on the explanation of why science in the Muslim world went into decline (some would say stagnation), nor even as to precisely when the decline began, although almost all would agree that it began sometime between the eleventh and sixteenth centuries.[310] It was not an abrupt phenomenon, but took place gradually and unevenly. Even after the scope and frequency of scientific enterprise had fallen far from its peak, there were pockets of activity. When Spain was falling to the Reconquista, parts of the Eastern Muslim world were still thriving. Taqi ad-Din Muhammad ibn Ma'ruf al-Rashid al-Dimashqi founded a great observatory in Istanbul with fifteen astronomers working under him in the 16th century and the magnificent Jai Singh Observatory in Delhi was built in the 18th century. By the twentieth century, however, there was not a single Muslim country with a major observatory.

Several suggestions have been advanced to explain this phenomenon. Among the suggestions are socio-politico-economic factors; political tyranny; invasion from outside forces such as the Mongols and the Crusaders; adoption of alien ideas; fanatical retention of obsolete ways; inherent problems in the religious law (e.g., failure to separate church and state or the legacy of sexism), inherent asymmetry between the East and West (e.g., precious metals, inbreeding, environmental degradation).[311]

---

[310] See Mohamad Abdalla, "The Fate of Islamic Science: A Review and Critique of Existing Theories and Opinions." Proceedings of the Conference on Arts and Humanities, Jan. 12-15, Honolulu, Hawaii, 2003.
http://www.hichumanities.org/AHproceedings/Mohamad%20Abdalla.pdf (accessed 8/30/03).

[311] Some of these ideas are discussed by Mohamed Abdulla, "The Fate of Islamic Science: A Review and Critique of Existing Theories and Opinions," others are discussed by Bernard Lewis, *What Went Wrong?* New York: Oxford University Press, 2002. See also Huff, Rise, p. 53.

Perhaps most of these have played some role in the decline of Islamic civilization, but I would argue that the possible exception of the hypothesized asymmetry between the East and West, every one of them becomes a problem, or at least a bigger problem, to the degree that *ijtihād* has been replaced by blind imitation (*taqlīd*). Thus, the loss of critical thinking, in addition to being a problem in-itself, has allowed the socio-politico-economic problems to fester unchallenged; left the Muslim world vulnerable to invasion from outside forces; deprived them of the ability to selectively adopt good alien ideas, as they did in the classical era; opened the door to the fanatical retention of obsolete ways; and crippled the once dynamic religious law. As to the inherent asymmetry between the East and West, I find it unconvincing. The Muslim world possesses 70% of the world's oil resources—an asymmetry in their favor. The meaningful asymmetry is that the West has embraced critical thinking at least since the Enlightenment while the Muslim world has either shunned it (in the case of the Sunnis) or reserved it to the domain of the religious elites (in the case of the Shi'a).

Islam, as described in the Qur'an, is a religion of tolerance, egalitarianism, and reason. As such, it provides a breeding ground for scientific progress, which thrives on such things. Scientific progress requires that the errors of one generation be rectified by the relentless questioning of the next. Everything must be open to question and debate. Nothing can be taken on blind faith (*taqlīd*); rather, it must be by clear proof (*tabayyun*). Islam is a religion of moderation. One does not see these principles practiced in the Muslim world today. We must, alas, make a distinction between the adjectives *Islamic* (what the religion teaches) and *Muslim* (what the people do). How did this situation come about?

History moves in a spiral rather than circles or a straight line. Although it repeats, over the long run there is some progress, some evolution. Certainly, scientific knowledge today is far beyond that

found in any earlier period. Ibn Khaldun, the father of modern sociol-
ogy, observed that history repeats itself in cycles of about 200 years.
During each period, a dynasty is born in the process of rejection of
the old dynasty; grows and prospers, becomes corrupt and declines,
and is rejected in turn and overthrown by revolution or by conquest in
revolution from the outside.

The first two centuries of Islam were an incubation period, beginning under the Prophet (peace be upon him) and the "Rightly-guided
Caliphs"[312] and ending in the revolution of the Sunni schools against
the politically intolerant *Mu`tazilah.*[313] It was during the reign of
Ma'mun, that the great surge in Islamic science began, with the found-
ing of the great observatories and universities as we have noted in the
previous chapters. Yet, though politically intolerant, the Mu'tazilah
were by no means ascetic, nor did they perceive scientific inquiry to be
a threat to their political authority.

Then from where did Islamic puritanism[314] come and why the fall
in Islamic scientific pre-eminence? I believe that European thought had
a reciprocal influence on the Muslim world during the same period that
Islamic thought was influencing Europe.[315] (Such reciprocal influence

---

[312] Title of the first four Caliphs.

[313] The *Mu'tazilah* were extreme rationalists who placed great emphasis on free will. They
called themselves the *ahl-al-adl wat-tawhîd* ("the Partisans of Justice and Unity"). They saw
man as the author of his own acts and held reason as the highest norm. By the early ninth
century, they had become the dominant school in Islam. In 827 the Mu'tazilite doctrine
was established as state dogma, however, in 833, they began a campaign to suppress those
who disagreed with them. They were overthrown by a coalition of schools less libertarian in
theory, but more tolerant in practice. This coalition, the progenitor of Sunni Islam, established
the intellectual tolerance (at least among one-another) that characterized the subsequent
centuries of the "Golden Era" of Islam.

[314] The journalist H. L. Menken described puritanism as "the haunting fear that someone,
somewhere may be happy."

[315] According to Nasr, *Science and Civilization*, Shihab-ad-Din as-Suhrawardi, the twelfth
century founder of the illuminist school of philosophy, argued that the real heaven begins at
the edge of the visible universe. A century later, at-Tusi, in his *Taṣawwurāt* (Notions), would
describe the views of the Shia Ismaili sect in words reminiscent of the Great Chain of Being,
which dominated medieval European theology.

has its analog in the world today as we see America increasing the power of its central government–even to the point of spying on its own citizens–at the moment that the former Soviet republics and Eastern Europe are turning to free markets).

The mechanism for this influence was the interplay of Sufi mysticism with Islamic orthodoxy. Al-Biruni's contemporary, Imam al-Ghazali, may have sown the seeds for the turnabout in Islamic fortunes. In his *Revival of the Religious Sciences*, al-Ghazali set up the reconciliation of Sufism and orthodox Islamic theology, with the objective of restoring a spiritual basis to the Islamic community.[316] In the process, however, what some have perceived as adulation of Sufi asceticism and scorn for the Aristotelian "philosophical school" may have had an unintended consequence.

The Sufis and their forerunners practiced asceticism and rejected materialism. The Hindu influence is obvious, but there are indications of Christian influence as well.[317] In addition to the body of traditions which associated Sufi thought with Muhammad, the Sufis also had a large store of traditions attributed to Jesus Christ (peace be upon them both). The latter, unless forged by Muslims, must have come from Christian sources and could be expected to reflect Christian attitudes on such issues as asceticism and knowledge. Until al-Ghazali, there had been a split between Sufism and orthodox Islam. Al-Ghazali, at the high point of Islamic science in the Arab world, reconciled Sufism and Islam by offering Sufi asceticism as an antidote for the materialistic excesses of Muslim rulers and the scholastic rationalism among the Islamic scholars. To al-Ghazali, a Sufi was merely an extremely conscientious Muslim whose God-consciousness was supreme over other desires and whose goal was to become fully God-reliant.

---

[316] Isma'il Raji al-Faruqi and Lois Lamya al-Faruqi, *The Cultural Atlas of Islam*. New York: MacMillan, 1986, 299 *ff.*

[317] See Javad Nurbakhsh, *Jesus in the Eyes of the Sufis*. London: Khaniqah-Nimutllahi Publ., 1982 for a discussion of Jesus from the Sufi viewpoint.

We have emphasized al-Ghazali's role in articulating the epistemology that underlies modern science. This epistemolgy is sometime called empiricism, but that is misleading, because, as we have noted before, the empirical route to knowledge is only one leg of the tripod of al-Ghazali's theory of knowledge. The reason for the overemphasis on empirical data is perhaps because it was the source of knowledge that got the least respect from the ancients, at least in the West. Al-Ghazali's respect for Sufism came from the realization that just as empirical knowledge is necessary for a scientific understanding of the real world, so the empirical experience of the Divine is necessary for one's knowledge of spiritual reality. Scripture may provide the authority for belief in God and the hereafter and reason may attest to its self-consistency, but without spiritual experience, we place our religious knowledge on a two-legged stool. We may BELIEVE in a religion based on scripture, and we may THINK that it is true based on our reason, but we do not KNOW the truth unless our experience supports it. It was the Sufis who offered a path to direct experience of the Divinity, just as the Muslim scientists had offered the empirical data in support of scientific knowledge.

This is the correct understanding of al-Ghazali's reconciliation of Sufism and orthodoxy. We can see the same parallels drawn in Ibn Tufail's *Awake the Son of Alive*,[318] which has been shown to have influenced John Locke.[319] In the light of this parallel, one might expect Sufi influence after al-Ghazali to be beneficial for the health of Islamic science. Why then does there seem to be a correlation between the migration of the centers of Islamic scientific research out of Baghdad, Persia, and North Africa to other existing hubs in Spain

---

[318] Lenn Evan Goodman, *Ibn Tufayl's Hayy ibn Yaqzan*. New York: Twain, 1972.

[319] G. A. Russell, "The Impact of the *Philosophus Autodidactus:* Pocockes, John Locke, and the Society of Friends," *The "Arabick" Interest of the Natural Philosophers in Seventeenth Century England. Brill's Studies in Seventeenth Century England*. Leiden: E. J. Brill, 1994, 224-265.

and India with influence of Sufism on the former locales?   The remaining islands of Islamic scientific brilliance in Spain, Sicily, and India eventually fell to the expansion of the newly revived European civilization into those areas. Thus, was the torch passed on.

> To those who inherit
> The earth in succession
> To its (previous) possessors,
> Is it not a guiding (lesson)
> That, if We so willed,
> We could punish them (too)
> For their sins, and [thus] seal up
> Their hearts so that they
> Could not hear?
> > – Qur'an (7:100)

I do not agree with those who argue that al-Ghazali was personally responsible for the decline of Islam. The astute reader will have noticed that every chapter of this book begins with a quote from al-Ghazali. He clearly included the natural sciences in the sphere of legitimate and necessary inquiry. Rather, I suggest that the reconciliation of Islam with Sufism in practice turned into a "slippery slope" that went beyond the restoration of the primacy of spiritual concerns over the material. More radical concepts such as the denial of matter and the elevation of asceticism to a virtue were able to slip in through the opened door as well. Islam rejects such notions.

> ... Islam does not regard the world as alien to righteousness
> or religious felicity. In itself, the world is not to be denied and
> combated. On the contrary, it is innocent and good, created
> precisely to the end of being used and enjoyed by man. The
> evil is not in it, but in its abuse by man. That is the villain
> which deserves to be denied and combated: the immoral use
> of the world. That is why the ethic of Islam is not that of

asceticism. The Prophet (peace be upon him) has directed his
followers against overextended rituals of worship, against
celibacy, against exaggerated fasting, against pessimism and
the morose mood.[320]

Of the Christian ascetics the Qur'an says:

... in the hearts of those who (truly) followed him [Jesus]
We engendered compassion and mercy. But as for monastic
asceticism–We did not enjoin it upon them: they invented it
themselves out of a desire for God's goodly acceptance. But
then they did not always observe it as it ought to have been
observed: and so we granted recompense unto such of them
as had (truly) attained to faith, whereas many of them
became iniquitous.

– Qur'an (57:27)
translated by Asad (1980) [321]

That al-Ghazali understood Sufism to mean moderation and
simplicity rather than extreme asceticism is implied by his use of
the founders of the four Sunni schools as models of Sufism.[322] None
of these men were ascetics in the monastic sense that is the subject
of the Qur'anic verse quoted above. Yet, once the attack on material indulgence had begun, there was no limit to it and the pendulum
swung completely in the other direction.

---

[320] Isma'il Raji al-Faruqi, *Tawḥīd: It's Implications for Thought and Life*. Kuala Lampur:
Dicetak oleh Percetakan Polygraphic Sdn. Bhd., 1982.

[321] Muhammad Asad, *The Message of the Qur'an* (Gibralter: Dar-al-Andalus, 1980). I have
used Asad's translation here because it seems closer to the original. The message is the same
in Ali's reading, and even more strongly emphasized: "... the Monasticism which they invented for themselves, We did not prescribe for them: (We commanded) only the seeking for the
Good Pleasure of God...."–Qur'an (57:27).

[322] al-Ghazali, *Ihya*, 40*ff*. Al-Ghazali even lists Solomon as an example of a Sufi because of his
commitment to charity, p. 46.

After praising mathematics, logic, and Sufism, al-Ghazali attacked what he characterized as the fourth branch of science:

> The fourth subject is Physics of which some portions contradict the Shariat and true religion and thus are not right.[323]

Aristotelian physics, which postulated two sets of laws instead of one for the universe, certainly contradicts the Qur'an and is also certainly not right. Yet, how can one, on the face of it, distinguish al-Ghazali's statement from the Catholic Church's objections to Bruno? Al-Ghazali's profound statement was not understood in the way most conducive to the continued progress of Islamic thought. It could have been the spur to a revolutionary physics such as we have seen in modern times. Instead, it was part of a legacy which closed the door to *ijtihād* and to innovative Islamic thought.

> The decline of science inside a great culture is in itself a fascinating study and a great object lesson. ... al-Ghazzāli famous eloquence ... went to building up the whirlwind of intolerance and blind fanaticism which tore down not only science but the very School system and the glorious *ijtihād*....[324]

It is ironic, given Sufism's emphasis on the primacy of spirit above legality, that in the aftermath of al-Ghazali's efforts Islamic jurisprudence was robbed of its dynamic element. *ijtihād*, the individual struggle for understanding, was replaced by *taqlīd*, blind imitation of the past.

> Islamic law, the product of an essentially dynamic and creative process, now tended to become fixed and institutionalized. While individual scholars like Ibn Taymiyya

---

[323] al-Ghazali, *Ihya*, vol. 1, 39.

[324] Giorgio de Santillana 1966, Preface, Nasr, *Science and Civilization.*

(*d.* 1328) and al-Suyuti (*d.* 1505) demurred, the majority
position resulted in traditional belief prohibiting substantive
legal development. This is commonly referred to as the
closing of the gate or door of *ijtihād*. Belief that the work of
the law schools had definitively resulted in the transforma-
tion of the Sharia [Islamic law] into a legal blueprint for
society reinforced the sacrosanct nature of tradition; change
or innovation came to be viewed as an unwarranted deviation (*bid'a*) from established sacred norms. To be accused
of innovation–deviation from the law and practice of the
community–was equivalent to the charge of heresy in
Christianity.[325]

Aversion to innovation is, of course, fatal to science. By the
fifteenth century the effect of the closing of the door to *ijtihād* on
scientific progress in the Islamic world was unmistakable.

In this book, I have sought to show how the seven factors that
I enumerated in Chapter 3, were responsible for Islam's golden era
of scientific progress. What is the status of these factors in the
Muslim world today?

(1) *Induction*. The persistent confusion over the Islamic calendar
shows that there is an inadequate understanding of induction in the
Muslim world. The insistence on requiring actual moonsightings and
then uncritically accepting false reports suggests the crudest sort of
empiricism.

(2) *Universality*. Any renaissance of Islamic science will require
the critical incorporation of modern Western knowledge into the new
Islamic knowledge, just as the early Muslims freely evaluated numerous foreign bodies of knowledge. Today's Muslims have not yet
demonstrated that they accept this. Instead, there is still an undertone
of feeling that everything in the West is bad and must be rejected in

---

[325] John L. Esposito, *Islam: The Straight Path*. New York: Oxford University Press, 1988, 85.

toto. No greater insult can be hurled by one Muslim against another than to say: You have been influenced by the West. Yet, in some important respects, America is more true to Islamic principles than some self-righteous societies in the Muslim world–not least of all in science.

(3) *Absence of a priesthood*. Iqbal's call for reopening the door to *ijtihād*–to "all qualified Muslims and not just the ulama[326] has not yet been heeded. With political power concentrated in the hands of a few, an elite group of jurists or clerics in their pay dictate how God's commands are to be applied to the modern world, and what knowledge may be pursued and what may not. This is effectively a priesthood as far as the prospects for scientific progress are concerned.[327]

(4) *Material success*. In the presence of the glorification of asceticism and, often, in the absence of economic freedom, the material prosperity that allows the support of pure scientific research is not possible. To the degree that Muslims take pride in their poverty, they have a disincentive against its alleviation.

(5) *Academic freedom*. The discussion in the previous chapter is only the tip of the iceberg regarding the paucity of academic freedom in the Muslim world. The absence of academic freedom is part of a general absence of freedom of expression in the Muslim world today.[328]

---

[326] Esposito, *Islam: The Straight Path*, 142-143.

[327] There is an analogy in the Marxist world. Stalinist Russia had no priests in positions of authority. But the Lysenko affair showed how the concentration of political and economic power in the hands of the state defeats the processes of inductive science. Under the centrally controlled scientific establishment, Lysenko's vague and untenable theories literally forced out sounder views because of the esthetically attractive (to Marxists) principle it espoused: that environment can directly alter hereditary traits.

[328] According to Freedom House only 30% of the 46 Muslim countries evaluated had a free or partly free press compared to 72% of 141 non-Muslim countries. Only one Muslim country (Mali) was deemed to have a completely free press compared to 74 non-Mulism countries. Cited by Neil Seeman, "Measuring a Free Press," *Fraser Forum* Oct. 2003, 18.

(6) *Citation.* I have already addressed this subject at length, but let me add one more example to drive home the point that proper citation has become a lost art. There is a book called *Glimpses of the Hadith* that goes into great detail describing the care early hadith compilers took in citing their sources.[329] The author, however, concludes with a lengthy list of alleged hadith for which he gives no citation whatsoever! In fact, some of them are not authentic hadith at all and the collection must be considered merely a compilation of Islamic proverbs. To determine which are authentic hadith would require what would be practically an original research effort on the part of the reader. In contrast to the early hadith compilations, this provides a poor model for scientific citation.[330] Modern Muslims appear to fear that critical examination of hadith literature will threaten long-cherished beliefs. The scientific model is to be ruthlessly critical in the hopes that any error, its longevity notwithstanding, will give way to truth.

(7) *Emphasis on learning and study.* This is the one area where attitudes are beginning to change. Unfortunately, the motivation seems to be the ignoble one of envy of the West's greater imperial power. I have met many students from Muslim countries and their attitude is too often a desire to learn engineering and urban planning but to avoid getting contaminated by any notions of independent or original thought. This will not do. Scientific progress does not consist of mere imitation of the products of technology. Learning and study must include a reopening of *ijtihād.* Scientific research will require total freedom of thought, experiment, and discussion: all of the elements of induction.

---

[329] Muhammad Azizullah, *Glimpses of the Hadith. Takoma Park, MD. Crescent Publications,* 1972.

[330] It does, however, follow the pattern of Al-Ghazali. While I think that Ghazali's anti-rationalism has been unfairly exaggerated, his habit of attributing quotations to the Prophet without citing his sources set a very bad precedent. The willingness of the Muslim community to accept these unsubstantiated attributions is yet another signal of the incipient decline of Islamic science coincident with Al-Ghazali's influence.

The vanishing or erosion of these factors in Muslim society cannot be laid at the feet of Islam itself which initially and for a very long period inspired them. For example, the claim that Islam opposes logic because it is a foreign or useless science is absurd.[331] One should not confuse opposition to the now discredited view that pure reason is a sufficient guide to knowledge with the absurd claim that logic is useless or that its rules are invalid because non-Arabs conceived them.

By the same token, it would be misleading to say that the notion that sophisticated demonstrative arguments will only lead the masses astray is an "Islamic" notion because it was made respectable by Ibn Taymiyyah.[332] The notion was earlier advanced by the Greek-inspired Ibn Rushd's who used it against the orthodox al-Ghazali for making public arguments that, in Ibn Rushd's view should only be discussed among the elites.[333]

Similarly, the denigration of material success finds no support in the source texts of Islam or mainstream Islamic thought. This renunciation of the world is a later development due to Sufi influence.[334]

The educational system in the Muslim world today has been correctly criticized for its treatment of knowledge as a static body of facts. Students are encouraged to acquire knowledge by the memorization of facts with no attempt to inculcate or develop the ability for critical thought. That is, there is no encouragement to question or to even understand in a profound way the facts that are

---

[331] Huff, *Rise*, 68, attributes this piece of nonsense to the famous German scholar of Islam Ignaz Goldhizer.

[332] Huff, *Rise*, 67.

[333] Ibn Rushd, *The Book of the Decisive Treatise Determining the Connection Between the Law and Wisdom*, Charles E. Butterworth, trans. (Provo, UT: Brigham Young Univ. Press, 2001) 19-22.

[334] See, e.g., the analysis of Muhammad Aziz Lahbabi, *Le Personnalisme Musulman* (Paris 1964) summarized by Ibrahim M. Abu-Rabi, *Intellectual Origins of Islamic Resurgence in the Modern Arab World* (Albany: SUNY, 1996), 32-33.

presented. Critics, however, are mistaken when they consider that this approach to education, or at a more fundamental level, this conception of knowledge, is inherently Islamic.[335] We have shown the contrary, that in the Qur'an and in the practice of Muslims in the early period knowledge is to be questioned. Further, the development of hadith studies is predicated on suspicion of the reliability of transmission of source material and a desire to authenticate its validity by sound scholarly methodology. The replacement of the original educational model that made Islamic society productive with the later model that survives today was an innovation that, in my opinion, was the natural educational accessory to the politically motivated replacement of *ijtihād* by *taqlīd*.

The fact that the development of *taqlīd* is a late development contradicting the essential teachings of the Qur'an is critical. As late as the 15th century "the Egyptian scholar al-Suyūṭī (1445-1505) prided himself on how many subjects he had treated which no one before him had dealt with."[336] Yet, Toby Huff accurately describes the state of the Muslims world over the past several centuries when he asserts: "Both theology and law specifically rejected the idea of a rational agency attributable to all men in favor of the view that man should follow the path of tradition, of traditional authority (*taqlīd*), and not attempt to fathom the mysteries of external nature or sacred writ."[337] Had this been the case in the early Islamic era there would not have been the scientific developments that we know took place. Further, rather than discourage scientific study, the Qur'an actively encourages the study of God's signs and

---

[335] See, e.g., Huff, *Rise*, 75*ff*, especially 142: "[T]he believer is in no way empowered, much less authorized, to add anything to (or subtract anything from) the body of knowledge, for the consensus of the scholars has already perfected our knowledge of fiqh and the Shari'a. It is not up to mankind to innovate (which in religious affairs is equivalent to heresy) when understanding fails. At this point belief turns to taqlid, acceptance of the authority of tradition."

[336] Hodgson, *Venture* 2, 437.

[337] Huff, *Rise*, 116.

urges us to search for "flaws." From the time of the Mongol conquests, however, Islamic education aimed at the conservation of tradition rather than the inspiration of critical thinking.[338]

But that was then and this now. Today it is the West that has wholeheartedly adopted the inductive method. However, it has divorced itself from the inspirational roots at its foundation. At the 1991 meeting of the International Astronomers Union, I heard a speaker talk about the mass extinctions in earth's history.[339] He kept saying "Nature wants" and "Nature prepares," where a Muslim astronomer from the classical era would have said "God wants" and "God prepares."

Hearing him, I reflected on Thomas Jefferson's famous phrase about "the laws of Nature and Nature's God." Jefferson wanted to establish that there were eternal laws that governed men. He seemed to fear that if he attributed such laws to Nature's God alone rather than perhaps to Nature itself, that he would lose part of his intended audience.

That was in 1776. In the nineteenth century, secularism began to outpace religion. The publication of Henry David Thoreau's "Essay on Civil Disobedience" coincided with the publication of Karl Marx's *Communist Manifesto*. The former, declared man's direct responsibility to God and called for resistance to the State in order to bring about an end to the enslavement of some men by others. The latter denied God's existence and dismissed the possibility of moral action altogether in favor of submission to an economically based historical determinism in order to establish a dictatorship of the proletariat. As the pietist Protestants in America were approaching their most

---

[336] Hodgson, *Venture* 2, pp. 437*ff*.

[337] At certain moments in earth's geological history there have been extinctions of species of life on a massive scale. The disappearance of the dinosaurs is a notable case in point. For an Islamic perspective on these matters see Maurice Buccaille, *What Is the Origin of Man?* Paris: Seghers, Ninth Edition 1983.

spectacular victory (the abolition of slavery),[340] Marxism (which proposed the enslavement of all men to the State) was being born. Since
then, God's name has been heard with less frequency in both science
and political theory, with rather unhappy results. Yet, as I write these
words, that era seems to be ending. Signs of religious revival are every-
where and Marxist governments are collapsing around the world.

We live in an era in which scientific progress continues its expo-
nential growth. Where are the self-discipline and vision to go with it?
The impression that scientific knowledge is unlimited is exhilarating.
However, if it is not limited by moral conscience, the exhilaration
is heightened by an undercurrent of terror. It is like standing up on
a roller coaster ride. The absence of constraint adds to the thrill, but
is unwise in the extreme. As Warith Deen Muhammad succinctly
put it: "Freedom without vision is destruction."[341] Scientific progress
without a moral vision can lead to destruction on a massive scale.
Consider Hiroshima and Nagasaki.

Islam is reawakening, but struggling for its bearings, seeking its
equilibrium. The colonial era was a period when Muslims embraced
asceticism and fatalism and left the material world to the West. Yet, the
result of the embrace of the asceticism that the West had abandoned
and the desertion of science has not been the establishment a spiritual
paradise. Instead, the Muslim world woke to find Palestine in the hands
of secularized European colonists; most of the Islamic world as client
states of secular or atheist superpowers; and the rest in the hands of
oppressive regimes believed by their subjects, rightly or wrongly, to be
practitioners of hypocrisy. What is undeniable is that the scientific
research in those countries can in no way be compared to the classical
Islamic civilization described in this book.

---

[340] "In Britain and America, the Quakers, who began their criticism in 1671, were the first
significant opponents of slavery, and the dynamics of the antislavery movement were largely
religious throughout". See Philip W., Goetz, *et al.* "Slavery, Serfdom, and Forced Labor," in
the *Encyclopaedia Britannica, Macropaedia,* v. 16.

[341] At a lecture at Howard University (c. 1978).

There is nothing wrong with the genes of the Muslim people. There are individual Muslims doing sound scientific research today. Their tendency to be located in the West or in those Muslim countries less repressive in academic matters should not be surprising in the light of what we have said here. How, then, can one of the richest nations in the world ignore the fact that it once accepted the sighting of a new moon hours before a solar eclipse was observed by millions in Europe? Solar eclipses only occur *before* the sighting of the new moon crescent is possible. This is an undisputed fact as certain to any astronomer as the fact that the earth is round.

Clearly, there is a flaw in the system at work here. The problem with too many Muslims is that they will read a book on the glories of the bygone Islamic civilization and pat themselves on the back as to how great Islam is. Neither the greatness of the Qur'an nor the holiness of the Prophet are of use to a people who neither understand nor put into practice the principles they advanced.

The golden era of Islam was an era of tolerance, of freedom, and of a deep love for the pursuit of knowledge. It was an era in which it was understood that ALL knowledge is religious knowledge. There is no sacred and no profane.

Al-Ghazali was correct to reject astrology as incompatible with Islam, but that did not mean that the Muslim was to reject it blindly. It did not mean that the books of astrology were to be burned or its practitioners persecuted. That was, and remains, the road to ignorance. All claims to knowledge must be freely available for study and review to be destroyed not by political persecution, but by measurement on the balance of truth–that is to say, by the inductive method which Muslims have abandoned.

Modern Muslim states have shown little interest in inductive research and free debate. They are more interested in the suppression of debate. All so-called "Muslim" governments engage in censorship and banning of books, etc. The use of such direct coercion is difficult outside the territory under their jurisdiction, of course. Muslims who immigrate to the West can bring their inhibitions against questioning authority with them, however. Deception is a more expedient mechanism than coercion for the suppression of ideas in non-Muslim countries. In the previous chapter I gave an example from my personal experience.[342]

There must be no limit to the general rule that our understanding must be tested openly and freely. There is no other way to attain knowledge. Islam itself has spread by competition in the open marketplace against other religions. Nor has it ever been preserved save by that method. Repression and fraud are impediments to knowledge, never their facilitators.

> O ye who believe!
> Stand out firmly For justice, as witnesses
> To God, even as against
> Yourselves, or your parents,
> Or your kin, and whether
> It be (against) rich or poor:
> For God can best protect both.
> – Qur'an (4:135)

---

[342] There is also the case of the "New Revised Edition" of Abdullah Yusuf Ali's translation of and commentary on the Qur'an (amana: Beltsville, 1989). The commentary in this "edition" is not so much revised as censored. The Publisher's Note places responsibility for the work on anonymous "scholars" and "committees." The only scholar named by the publisher is the late Isma'il al-Faruqi who was assassinated in 1986, long before the book was published, and who, therefore, cannot explain why he would have acquiesced to such revisions as, for example, the removal of Yusuf Ali's appendices on the "Allegorical Interpretation of the Story of Joseph," "Mystic Interpretation of the Verse of Light," and "The Muslim Heaven" from the "New Revised Edition." Buyers of what is called "Ali's" translation and commentary are unwittingly deprived of Ali's actual work and ideas. Proper attention to citation such as we have discussed in this book would require that the scholars who passed judgment on Yusuf Ali's commentary identify themselves in print and make their criticisms openly. When Imam Muslim put out his hadith compilation, he did not call it the "New Revised" edition of the *Sahīh Bukhari*! As we have said before, academic scholarship must be done openly. For a more detailed discussion of this matter, see Imad A. Ahmad, "On the 'New Revised Edition' of Yusuf Ali's Qur'anic Translation," *Reminder* 4 (1992): # 2, http://theamericanmuslim.org/tam.php/features/articles/book_review_on_the_new_revised_edition_of_yusuf_alis_quranic_translation/ (accessed 1/29/06).

Some may argue that the government of a country whose population remains 100% Muslim deserves credit, notwithstanding its repression. Any credit for the people's fidelity to Islam belongs to Islam and not to the regimes that oppress them. After all, Muslim countries have remained Muslim under repressive non-Muslim rulers as well. The essence of Islam lies not in the outward observance or facilitation of rituals, but in the holy struggle (*jihād*) to establish justice.

> Do ye make the giving
> Of drink to pilgrims,
> Or the maintenance of
> The Sacred Mosque, equal
> To (the pious service of) those
> Who believe in God
> And the Last Day, and strive
> With might and main
> In the cause of God?
>   – Qur'an (9:19)

When the Prophet urged his companions to "help your brother whether he was the oppressor or ... the oppressed," they asked how they could help an oppressor? He replied: "By preventing him from oppressing."[343] A country may call itself Muslim merely because its population professes Islam. But is it truly Islamic if it cannot withstand free comparison to competing ideology? If it cannot compute the date of a Muslim holiday? What would al-Ghazali say?[344]

> The Prophet said: The learned are the representatives of the people while they do not mix with the rulers. When they mix, they commit treachery to the prophets. So beware of

---

[343] *Sahih Bukhari*, 3:623, 624; 4:358, 9:84.

[344] Although Al-Ghazali attributes these sentiments here to the Prophet, he provides no citation, so that I must call the view his rather than those of the Prophet, although the Prophet may have agreed with them.

them and don't mix with them. Hazrat Sayeed-b-Musayyeb said: When you see a learned man frequenting the house of a ruler, beware of his company as he is a thief. Hazrat Aozayi [sic] said: There is nothing more hateful to God than a learned man who frequents the house of a ruler. The Prophet said: The learned men who frequent the houses of rulers are worst and the rulers who frequent the houses of learned men are best.[345]

Compare this to the American situation, where almost absolute freedom of religion has made Islam the fastest growing religion. Contrast the pride with which American converts to Islam talk about their new religion with the guilt which many immigrants from Muslim countries exhibit. The majority of immigrants avoid letting anyone know their religious affiliation—even to the point of men skipping prayers when they might be observed and women removing their headscarf despite their own personal conviction that it is mandatory in public.

> Let there be no compulsion
> In religion: Truth stands out
> Clear from Error: whoever
> Rejects Evil and believes
> In God hath grasped
> The most trustworthy
> Hand-hold, that never breaks.
> And God heareth
> And knoweth all things.
> 　　　　　 – Qur'an (2:256)

---

[345] al-Ghazali, *Ihya*, vol. 1, 87-88.

The willingness of Muslims to resolve the confusion over the calendar is a litmus test of their willingness to resume a leadership position on scientific questions in general.

> ... Verily never
> Will God change the condition
> Of a people until they
> Change it themselves
> (With their own souls).
>
> – Qur'an (13:11)

An Islamic renaissance IS possible. It will occur when a knowledgeable faith in God replaces blind faith in tradition, when tolerance replaces puritanism, when free inquiry replaces repression, when love of truth replaces love of material wealth, when realization of the transcendence of God replaces mindless mysticism. Some may shake their heads and say that these things will never happen. They do not know the power of God, Who turns towards man again and again. In the Qur'an, the doctrine of the resurrection is supported by the following argument: How can any one doubt that the God Who made man in the first place can make him again? Similarly, I ask, if the original Islamic scientific civilization is possible, why doubt that another can arise?

God knows the intention in my heart. May He forgive me for my errors, and may He forgive us all. I have written what I have written, and I seek God's forgiveness.

> God intends every facility
> For you, He does not want
> To put you to difficulties.
>
> – Qur'an (2:185)

But if they turn away,
Thy duty is only to preach
The Clear Message.

They recognize the favours
Of God; then they deny them;
And most of them
Are (creatures) ungrateful.

  – Qur'an (16:82-83)

The Prophet said: The ignorance of an ignorant man is more harmful than the transgression of a sinner. On the Resurrection Day a man will be raised to the rank of nearness to God in proportion to his intellect. The Prophet said: Nobody earns a better thing than intellect. It shows him the path towards guidance and saves him from destruction.... [W]hen his intellect becomes perfect he obeys God and disobeys his enemy the devil. The Prophet said: Every thing has a root and the root of a believer is his intellect. Have you not heard the words of the sinners in Hell: Had we heard and understood, we would not have been the inmates of Hell.–al Ghazali[346]

---

[346] al-Ghazali, *Ihya*, vol. 1, 111.

Figure 9
Jai Singh Observatory, Built in 18th Century Delhi on the Model of the
Classical Islamic Observatories of Maragha and Samarkand
(by Roland and Sabrina Michaud, Woodfin Camp & Associates)

Verily, all things have We created
In proportion and measure.
– Qur'an (54:49)

BIBLIOGRAPHY

Abdus Salam. *Unification of Fundamental Forces: The First of the 1988 Dirac Memorial Lectures*. New York: Cambridge Univ. Press, 1990.

Ahmad, Imad A. *"Al-Biruni Commemorative Volume." (review), Archeoastronomy*, vol. V #1 (Jan.-March 1982): 40.

Ahmad, Imad A. "Did Muhammad Witness a Canterbury Swarm?" *Bulletin of the American Astronomical Society,* 19 (1988): 1011.

Ahmad, Imad A. "The Dawn Sky on Lailat-ul-qadr (the Night of Power)." *Bulletin of the American Astronomical Society,* 21 (1989): 1217.

Ahmad, Imad A. *A Uniform Islamic Calendar for the Western Hemisphere (411 A.H.-1413 A.H.)*. Bethesda: Imad-ad-Dean, Inc., 1990.

Ahmad, Imad A. "On the 'New Revised Edition' of Yusuf Ali's Qur'anic Translation," *Reminder* 4 (1992): # 2. (http://theamericanmuslim.org/tam.php/features/articles/book_review_on_the_new_revised_edition_of_yusuf_alis_quranic_translation/ (accessed 1/29/06).

Ahmad, Imad A. "Islamic Contributions to Scientific Methods," *The Journal of Faith and Science Exchange* IV (2000): 27-30.

Ahmad, Imad A. ed. *Proceedings of the IIIT Lunar Calendar Conference, 2nd ed.* Herndon: IIIT, 1998.

Ahmad, Nafis. "Some Glimpses of Al-Bīrūnī as a Geographer." In *Al-Bīrūnī Commemorative Volume: Proceedings of the International Congress Held in Pakistan*. ed. H. M. Said. Karachi: Hamdard, 1979.

Ali, Jamil. The Determination of the Coordinates of Cities, *Al-Bīrūnī's Taḥdīd al-Amākin*. Beirut: Centenniel Publ. Univ. of Beirut, 1967.

Amico, Giovanni Battista. *On the Motions of the Heavenly Bodies according to Peripatetic Principles without Eccentrics or Epicycles*. Venice, 1536.

Arnaldez, Roger. "The Theory and Practice of Science According to ibn Sina and Al-Bīrūnī." In *Al-Bīrūnī Commemorative Volume: Proceedings of the International Congress Held in Pakistan*. ed. H. M. Said. Karachi: Hamdard, 1979.

Arnold, T. W. 1913. *The Preaching of Islam: A History of the Propagation of the Muslim Faith*. Lahore: Ashraf, 1961.

Aquinas, St. Thomas 1269. *Summa Theoligica*, Part 1, ques. 32, quoted by Polanyi (1958).

Asin, Miguel. *Islam and the Divine Comedy*. New Delhi: Goodword, 2001.

Asad, Muhammad. *The Message of the Qur'an*. Gibralter: Dar-al-Andalus, 1980.

Azizullah, Muhammad. *Glimpses of the Hadith*. Takoma Park, MD: Crescent Publications, 1972.

Barani, S. H. "Al-Biruni's Scientific Achievements." *Indo-Iranica*, 5 (1952): #4.

Bartlett, John. *Bartlett's Familiar Quotations*. Boston: Little Brown, 1980.

Benz, Ernst W. "Christianity." In the *Encyclopaedia Britannica, Macropaedia*, v. 4. Chicago: Encyclopaedia Britannica, Inc., 1980.

Bowker, John *The Religious Imagination and the Sense of God*. Oxford: Oxford Univ. Press, 1978.

Broad, C. D. 1951. "Bacon and the Experimental Method." In Lindsay, Jean, *A Short History of Science: Origins and Results of the Scientific Revolution*. New York: Anchor, 1959.

Brecher, K. *Bulletin of the American Astronomical Society*. 16 (1984): 476.

Bruno, Giordano 1584. *De'l Infinito Universo e Mondi*. in Singer, Dorothea Waley. *Giordano Bruno: His Life and Thought*. New York: Greenwood Press, 1950.

Buccaille, Maurice. *The Bible, Qur'an and Science*. Paris: Seghers, 1981.

Buccaille, Maurice. *What Is the Origin of Man?* Ninth Edition, Paris: Seghers, 1983.

Bultmann, Rudolph. *Theology of the New Testament*. tr. by K. Grobel, London: SCM Press, 1958.

Bunkowska, Barbara. "From Negation to Acceptance." In *The Reception of Copernicus' Heliocentric Theory*. Dordrecht: D. Reidel, 1972.

Carlyle, Thomas. *Heroes and Hero Worship*. Chicago: A.C. McClurg & Co., 1897.

Cobb, Stanwood. *Islamic Contributions to Civilization*. Washington, DC: Avalon Press, 1963.

Copernicus, Nicolaus 1543, *On the Revolutions of the Heavenly Spheres*. tr. by Charles Glenn Wallis, in *Britannica Great Books*, v. 16. Chicago: Encyclopaedia Britannica, Inc., 1980.

Crombie, A. C. *Science, Optics, and Music in Medieval and Early Modern Thought*. London: Hambledon, 1990.

Dallal, Ahmad Salim, *The Astronomical Work of Sadr al-Shai'ah: An Islamic Response to Greek Astronomy*. Ann Arbor: University Microfilms International, 1990.

Darwin, Bernard, *The Oxford Dictionary of Quotations*, 2nd Edition. London: Oxford University Press, 1959.

Davies, Paul, *The Mind of God: The Scientific Basis for a Rational World*. New York: Simon and Schuster, 1992.

de Santillana, Giorgio 1966. Preface to Nasr, Seyyed Hossein. *Islamic Science: An Illustrated Study*. London: World of Islam Festival Publ. Co., 1976.

de Santillana, Giorgio. "Galileo." in the *Encyclopaedia Britannica, Macropaedia*, v. 7. Chicago: Encyclopaedia Britannica, Inc., 1980.

Debarnot, Marie-Thérèse. "The Zij of Ḥabash al-Ḥāsib: A Survey of MS Istanbul Yeni Cami 784/2." In *From Deferent to Equant: A Volume of Studies in the History of Science in the Ancient and Medieval Near East in Honor of E. S. Kennedy*. eds. David A. King and George Saliba. New York: New York Academy of Sciences, 1987.

Denny, Frederick M. and Taylor, Rodney L. *The Holy Book in Comparative Perspective*. Columbia, SC: Univ. S. Carolina, 1985.

Draper, John William. *A History of the Intellectual Development of Europe* 2 vols. New York: Harper & Brothers, 1876.

Dreyer, J. L. E. 1906. *A History of Astronomy from Thales to Kepler,*
    2nd edition. New York: Dover, 1953.

Einstein, Albert. *Out of My Later Years.* New York: Philosophical Library, 1950.

Einstein, Albert. *Relativity: The Special and the General Theory: A Popular
    Exposition.* New York: Crown, 1961.

Esposito, John L. *Islam: The Straight Path.* New York: Oxford University Press,
    1988.

al-Faruqi, Isma'il Raji. *Christian Ethics: A Historical and Systematic Analysis
    of Its Dominant Ideas.* Montreal: McGill University Press, 1967.

al-Faruqi, Isma'il Raji. *Tawhīd: It's Implications for Thought and Life,*
    (Kuala Lampur: Dicetak oleh Percetakan Polygraphic Sdn. Bhd.). 1982.

al-Faruqi, Isma'il Raji and al-Faruqi, Lois Lamya. *The Cultural Atlas of Islam.*
    New York: MacMillan, 1986.

Flammarion, Camille, *L'Atmosphere.* Paris: Library Hachette, 1888.

Fort, Charles 1919. *The Book of the Damned.* New York: Holt, Reinhardt and
    Winston, 1941.

Frazer, James George 1922. *The Golden Bough.* New York: American Book-
    Stanford Press 1940.

Fuller, R. Buckminster, "Einstein." in *Cosmography: A Posthumous Scenario for
    the Future of Humanity.* New York: Macmillan, 1992

Galilei, Galileo 1614, "Letter to the Grand Duchess Christine of Lorraine."
    quoted by Henry Crew and Alfonso de Salvio in *Biographical Note in
    Britannica Great Books,* v. 28. Chicago: Encyclopaedia Britannica, Inc.

Gardet, Louis, "Portraits of Two Savants and Humanists–Bīrūnī and Albert the
    Great." in *Al-Biruni Commemorative Volume: Proceedings of the
    International Congress Held in Pakistan.* ed. H. M. Said. Karachi:
    Hamdard, 1979.

al-Ghazali 1106-1111, *Al-Ghazzali's Ihya Ulum-id-Din,* 4 vols. Al-Haj Maulana
    Fazul-ul-Karim, trans. Lahore: Book Lovers Bureau, 1971.

al-Ghazali c. 1100 in *The Faith and Practice of Al-Ghazzālī*. Montgomery Watt, *trans*. Liverpool: Tinling, 1953.

al-Ghazali c. 1095 in Al-Ghazali's *Tahāfūt Al-Falāsifah [Incoherence of the Philosophers]*. Sabih Ahmad Kamali, trans., Lahore: Sheikh, 1963.

Gibbon, Edward 1776. *The Decline and Fall of the Roman Empire*, volume I. in *Britannica Great Books*, v. 40. Chicago: Encyclopaedia Britannica, Inc., 1952.

Gingerich, Owen. "Was Ptolemy a Fraud?" *Quarterly Journal Royal Astronomical Society* 21 (1980): 253.

Gingerich, Owen. "Ptolemy Revisited: A Reply to R. R. Newton." *Quarterly Journal Royal Astronomical Society* 22 (1981): 40.

Gingerich, Owen. "The Origins of Ptolemy's *Astronomical Parameters*," *(Review) Journal History of Astronomy* 21 #4 (1990): 364.

Gingerich, Owen. "Islamic Astronomy." *Scientific American*, 254 #10 (April 1986): 74.

Goetz, Philip W., et al. "Slavery, Serfdom, and Forced Labor." in the *Encyclopaedia Britannica, Macropaedia*, v. 16. Chicago: Encyclopaedia Britannica, Inc., 1980.

Goodman, Lenn Evan. *Ibn Tufayl's Hayy ibn Yaqzān*. New York: Twain, 1972.

Hahn, Roger. "Laplace and the Mechanistic Universe." In Lindberg, David C. and Numbers, Ronald L. *God and Nature*. Berkeley: U. of California Press, 1986.

Hamarneh, Sami K. "The Life Sciences." in *The Genius of Arab Civilization: Source of Renaissance*. ed. John Richard Hayes. (Swith City Publisher) Cambridge: MIT Press, 1978.

Hart, Michael H. *The One Hundred: A Ranking of the Most Influential Persons in History*. New York: Hart, 1978.

Harvey, William. *An Anatomical Disquisition on the Motion of the Heart and Blood in Animals*. in *Britannica Great Books*, v. 28. Chicago: Encyclopaedia Britannica, Inc., 1952.

Haykal, Muhammad H. *The Life of Muhammad*. North American Trust, 1976.

Heath, Sir Thomas. *Aristarchous of Samos*. Oxford: Oxford University Press, 1913.

Hogendijk, Jan P. and AbdelHamid I. Sabra, *The Enterprise of Science in Islam: New Perspectives*. Cambridge, MS: MIT Press, 2003.

Hodgson, Marshall G.S. *The Venture of Islam: Conscience and History in a World Civilization vols. 1-3*. Chicago: University of Chicago Press, 1961.

Huff, Toby. *The Rise of Early Modern Science: Islam, China, and the West*. New York: Cambridge, 2003.

Ibn al-Haytham, c. 1000. *The Optics of Ibn Al-Haytham, Bk. I: On Direct Vision*. A.I. Sabra, trans. London: Warbug Institute, 1989.

Ibn Munqidh, Usamah. 12th c. *Memoirs of an Arab Syrian Gentleman or An Arab Knight in the Crusades*. trans. by Philip K. Hitti Beirut: Khayyats, 1964.

Ilyas, Muhammad. *Astronomy of Islamic Calendar*. Kuala Lampur: A. S. Noordeen, 1997.

Iqbal, Mohammad. *The Reconstruction of Religious Thought in Islam*. Lahore: S.M. Ashraf, 1944.

Jacob, Margaret C. "Christianity and the Newtonian Worldview." in Lindberg, David C. and Numbers, Ronald L. *God and Nature*. Berkeley: U. of California Press, 1986.

James, Edwin O. "Priesthood." in the *Encyclopaedia Britannica, Micropaedia*, v. 14. Chicago: Encyclopaedia Britannica, Inc., 1980.

Kennedy, Edward S. "The Arabic Heritage in the Exact Sciences." *Al Habath* 23 (1970): 327.

Kennedy, E.S. *A Commentary upon Bīrūnī's Kitāb Taḥdīd al-Am'kin*. Beirut: American Univ. of Beirut, 1973.

King, David A. and Saliba, George. *Eds. From Deferent to Equant: A Volume of Studies in the History of Science in the Ancient and Medieval Near East in Honor of E. S. Kennedy.* New York: New York Academy of Sciences, 1987.

Koyré, Alexandre. *The Astronomical Revolution.* Paris: Hermann, 1973.

Kremer, R. L. "Bernard Walthen's Astronomical Observations." *Journal History of Astronomy* 11 (1980): 174.

Kuhn, Thomas. *The Structure of Scientific Revolutions.* Chicago: Univ, of Chicago, 1970.

Lane, Rose Wilder 1997. *Islam and the Discovery of Freedom.* Beltsville, MD: amana, 1997.

Lindberg, David C. *Studies in the History of Medieval Optics.* London: Variorum Reprints, 1983.

Lindberg, David C. 1986, "Science and the Early Church," in Lindberg, David C. and Numbers, Ronald L. *God and Nature.*

Lindberg, David C. and Numbers, Ronald L. *God and Nature: Historical Essays on the Encounter Between Christianity and Science.* Berkeley: U. of California Press, 1986.

Marcorini, Edgardo. *The History of Science and Technology vol. 1.* New York: Facts on File, 1988.

Mirza, Mohamad R. and Siddiqi, Muhammad Iqbal. eds., *Muslim Contribution to Science*, Lahore: Kazi, 1986.

Mokyr, Joel. *The Lever of Riches: Technological Creativity and Economic Progress.* New York: Oxford University Press, 1990.

Morgan, J. *Mohametism Explained.* London: 1723-1725.

Nadwi, Abdullah Abbas. *Vocabulary of the Holy Qur'an.* Chicago: Iqra International Educational Foundation, 1983.

Nasr, Seyyed Hossein. *Islamic Science: An Illustrated Study.* London: World of Islam Festival Publ. Co., 1976.

Nasr, Seyyed Hossein. *Science and Civilization in Islam, 2nd ed.* Cambridge UK: Islamic Texts Society, 1987.

Newton, Isaac 1687. *Mathematical Principles of Natural Philosophy.* Andrew Motte, Revised by Florian Cajori, in *Britannica Great Books*, v. 34. Chicago: Encyclopaedia Britannica, Inc.

Newton, Robert R. *Ancient Astronomical Observations and the Accelerations of the Earth and Moon.* Baltimore: Johns Hopkins University, 1970.

Newton, Robert R. *The Crime of Claudius Ptolemy.* Baltimore: Johns Hopkins University, 1977.

Newton, Robert R. *The Origins of Ptolemy's Astronomical Parameters.* Baltimore: Johns Hopkins University, 1982.

Nurbakhsh, Javad. *Jesus in the Eyes of the Sufis.* London: Khaniqah-Nimutllahi Publ., 1982.

Paine, Thomas 1774. *The Age of Reason, in The Life and Major Writings of Thomas Paine.* ed. Philip S. Foner. Secaucus NJ: Citadel, 1974.

Pais, Abraham. *"Subtle Is the Lord–": the Science and the Life of Albert Einstein.* New Brunswick, NJ: Transaction Books, 1982.

Pannekoek, A. *A History of Astronomy.* London: George Allen and Unwin Unl., 1961.

Polanyi, Michael 1958. *Personal Knowledge: Towards a Post-Critical Philosophy.* Chicago: Univ. of Chicago Press, 1962.

Ptolemy, Claudius. c. 151, *The Almagest.* trans. by R. Catesby Taliaferro, in *Britannica Great Books*, v. 16. Chicago: Encyclopaedia Britannica, Inc.

Ragg, Lonsdale and Ragg, Laura. *The Gospel of Barnabus.* Cedar Rapids, IA: United Publishing, 1980.

Rashed, Roshdi. "Islam and the Flowering of the Exact Sciences." In *Islam, Philosophy, and Science.* Paris: United Nations, 1981.

Risvi, Saiyid Samad Husein. "Portraits of Two Savants and Humanists–Bīrūnī and Albert the Great." In *Al-Biruni Commemorative Volume:*

Proceedings of the International Congress Held in Pakistan. ed.
H. M. Said, Karachi: Hamdard, 1979.

Russell, Bertrand. *The Impact of Science on Society.* London: Allen & Unwin,
1952.

G. A. Russell, ed. *The "Arabick" Interest of the Natural Philosophers in
Seventeenth Century England. Brill's Studies in Seventeenth Century
England.* Leiden: E.J. Brill, 1994,

Sabra, AbdelHamid I. "The Exact Sciences." in *The Genius of Arab Civilization:
Source of Renaissance*, ed. John Richard Hayes. MIT Press:
Cambridge, 1978.

Sabra, Abdel Hamid I. "Ibn al-Haytham's Revolution Project in Optics. The
Achievement and the Obstacle." In *Enterprise in Islam.* ed. Hogendus,
Ian. P. and AbdelHamid I. Sabra. MIT Press: Cambridge, 2003.

Sachau, Edward C. *Alberuni's India.* New York: Norton & Co.. Inc., 1971.

Saliba, George. *A History of Arabic Astronomy: Planetary Theories During the
Golden Age of Islam.* New York: NYU, 1994.

Saliba, George. "The Height of the Atmosphere According to Mu'ayyad al-Dīn
al-Urdi, Qutb al-Dīn al-Shīrāzī, and Ibn Mu'ādh. *From Deferent to
Equant: A Volume of Studies in the History of Science in the Ancient
and Medieval Near East in Honor of E. S. Kennedy.* eds. David A. King
and George Saliba. New York: New York Academy of Sciences, 1987.

Saliba, George."Theory and Observation in Islamic Astronomy: The Work of Ibn
Al-Shātir of Damascus." *Journal History of Astronomy* 18 (1987): 35.

Sarton, George. *Introduction to the History of Science. I. From Homer to Omar
Khayyam.* Washington DC: Carnegie Institute of Washington, 1927.

Sarton, George. *Introduction to the History of Science. II. From Robert
Grosseteste to Roger Bacon.* Washington DC: Carnegie Institute of
Washington, 1931.

Sayili, Aydin M. *The Observatory in Islam.* NY: Arno, 1981.

Schacht, Joseph and Bosworth, C.E. *The Legacy of Islam.* Oxford: Clarendon,
1974.

Schaefer, Bradley E. "Heavenly Signs," *New Scientist* (21/28 December 1991).

Schneer, Cecil J. *The Search for Ideas: The Development of Ideas from the Earliest Times to the Present.* New York: Grove, 1960.

Siddiqi. 'Abdul Hamid. *Saḥīḥ Muslim.* Lahore: Ashraf, 1976.

Siddiqi, M. Razi-ud-Din. in *Muslim Contribution to Science.* eds. Mohamad R. Mirza and Muhammad Iqbal Siddiqi. Lahore: Kazi, 1986.

Singer, Dorothea Waley. *Giordano Bruno: His Life and Thought.* New York: Greenwood Press, 1950.

Snow, C. P. *The Two Cultures and the Scientific Revolution.* New York: Cambridge Univ. Press, 1959.

Stephenson, F. R., and Morrison, L. V. "Precision of Islamic Eclipse Measurements." *Journal History of Astronomy,* 22 (1991): 195.

Swerdlow, N. M., and Neugabauer, O. *Mathematical Astronomy in Copernicus's De Revolutionibus.* New York: Springer-Verlag, 1984.

Taton, René. *History of Science: Ancient and Modern Science from the Beginnings to 1450.* New York: Basic Books, 1963.

Thessleff, Holger. "Pythagorus." in the *Encyclopaedia Britannica, Macropaedia,* v. 15. Chicago: Encyclopaedia Britannica, Inc., 1980.

Westfall, Richard S. "The Rise of Science and the Decline of Orthodox Christianity: A Study of Kepler, Descartes, and Newton." In Lindberg, David C. and Numbers, Ronald L. *God and Nature.* Berkeley: U. of California Press, 1986.

White, Andrew Dickson. *A History of the Warfare of Science with Theology in Christendom,* 2 vols. New York: Appleton, 1896.

Whitman, Walt 1865. "When I Heard the Learned Astronomer." In *Leaves of Grass and Selected Prose,* ed. John Kouwnhoven. New York: Random House, 1950.

Zeilik, M. *Astronomy: The Evolving Universe,* 9th Edition. Cambridge: Cambridge, 2002

INDEX

A

Abraham viii, 13-15, 60, 69, 133, 137

Abrahamic message 16

Academic freedom 12, 154, 156, 179

Academy 86, 195, 198, 201

Africa 174

Africans 71

Agriculture 146

Ahmad, Imad-ad-Dean xviii, 30, 56, 61

Albert Magnus 23, 73

Alexandria 17, 41

Alfonsine Tables 120

Algebra 47, 74

Ali, A. Yusuf x, 162, 163, 176, 186

Almagest 72, 80, 104, 108, 110, 200

Almanacs 83, 147

America 153, 155, 179, 184

Anatomy 76, 161

Andromeda Galaxy 9

Aozayi 188

Apollo mission 64

Apsides, Line of 90

Aquinas, St. Thomas 23, 130

Arabic numerals 74

Arabs 19, 20, 45, 55, 59, 67, 71, 78, 127, 146, 181

Archimedes 7, 32

Architecture 47, 79

Aristarchos 119

Aristarchus 40, 82, 92

Aristotle 13, 19, 30, 31, 38, 71, 72, 95-97, 102-104, 109, 121, 125, 129

Arius 17, 25, 134

Aryabhata 119

Asceticism 3, 19, 20, 172, 175, 176, 179, 184

Astrolabe 117

Astrology 4, 60, 68, 69, 86, 154, 185

As-Sufi 83

As-Suhrawardi 172

Athanasian Creed 18

Athanasius 134

At-Tusi xv, 41, 86-88, 111, 113, 114, 120, 121

Augustine, Saint 128

Avempace 110